5

GW01445244

5
minute

SERMONS

for kids

from

Nature

Anne Pilmoor

Published in 2020 by Autumn House Publications (Europe) Ltd., Grantham, Lincolnshire, UK.

British Library Cataloguing in Publication Data. A catalogue record for this book is available from the British Library.

ISBN 978-1-78665-945-3

Designed by Abigail Murphy.
Printed in Serbia.

CONTENTS

INTRODUCTION

It is hoped that this book of *52 5-minute Sermons for Kids from Nature* will be a helpful resource for the church and the home. It is our prayer that, through these illustrations, children will gain broad information about the natural world they live in, coupled with promises, instructions and advice from the Bible that will find fertile ground in their hearts and minds. One of the aims of this book is to create a ready resource for busy pastors, lay preachers, teachers, storytellers, and parents, though the overarching aim is to create helpful stepping stones for our children to lead them along their own personal spiritual journeys.

The illustrations are short and factual; they should not be read, but freely presented with additions, comments and embellishments of your own. Obviously, information in the sermons will be selected and pitched to best suit the ages of the children. It is useful to bear in mind that young children have short attention spans. Try to bring in the suggested items in the 'You could use' sections and keep the story-telling short. A rule of thumb is three minutes for 3-year-olds, four minutes for 4-year-olds, and continue the pattern for the 5-and-more-year-olds. Where there are mixed ages, five minutes should be the absolute maximum.

Dedicated to Maja and Tom,
two precious jewels in His crown!

Anne Pilmoor

Something about Seeds

sermon 1

THEME

The size of the seed does not determine the size of the plant. No matter how small we may feel we are, we can grow while doing special work for Jesus.

BIBLE GEM

'Here is another illustration Jesus used: "The Kingdom of Heaven is like a mustard seed planted in a field. It is the smallest of all seeds, but it becomes the largest of garden plants; it grows into a tree, and birds come and make nests in its branches." ' *Matthew 13:31, 32 (NLT)*

YOU COULD USE

- Packets of different-sized seeds
- An orchid plant
- Some mustard seeds
- A coconut

ILLUSTRATION

Do any of you know which plant has the smallest seeds ever? I don't have one of its seeds. If I did, you'd need a magnifying glass to see it, because it is only 0.2mm in length! That's tiny! If you had one of those seeds and planted it in the right conditions, and you waited many months for it to germinate, you would finally end up with a beautiful orchid plant called *Aerides odorata*. (It belongs to the same family as the plant I have here.) The *Aerides odorata* grows all over China, South East Asia and the Philippines. Isn't it amazing that something so small can grow into something so beautiful?

Now, I wonder if you could tell me what the largest seed in the world might be? It is the coco de mer, sometimes called the double coconut or sea coconut. [Show the children the coconut but explain that the coco de mer is much larger.] The seed from the coco de mer palm grows only on two islands of the Seychelles, and sadly it is in danger of extinction. This seed can weigh up to twenty kilograms! That is about the same weight as each of the six-year-old boys and girls listening here!

Can you imagine a seed taking six years to mature and to be ready for planting, and then, once planted, taking another three to six months to germinate? That is how long it takes for the coco de mer to mature and then germinate!

In 1960 some very old date seeds were found near Masada on the edge of the Dead Sea. The scientists did tests on them and said they were about 2,000 years old. That would have been from the time when Jesus lived there. Three of the seeds were planted, but only one germinated and grew. That seed should be a thirteen-year-old tree by now. Isn't it wonderful that new life should burst forth from a seed that old?

Jesus told the story of the mustard seed. Mustard seeds are small, only one or two millimetres in diameter. Once planted, they can grow up to twenty feet tall (that is more than three six-foot-tall men from end to end) and twenty feet wide. The mustard tree is an evergreen shrub that birds enjoy nesting in. In this story Jesus explained that we only need a small amount of faith to do great things for Him. It doesn't matter that we may be a small seed. The important thing is that we are planted and grow in Him.

PRAYER

Dear Jesus, plant me in Your heart, where I can grow to be strong like You. Amen.

Baviaan, the Baboon sermon 2

THEME

We need to learn to be self-controlled and disciplined in many areas of our lives.

BIBLE GEM

'He must be hospitable, one who loves what is good, who is self-controlled, upright, holy and disciplined.' *Titus 1:8*

YOU COULD USE

- A toy baboon, or
- Photographs of baboons – single and in a troop

ILLUSTRATION

When I was young, I lived close to a mountain. It was a beautiful mountain which we loved to climb. There were lots of different birds, and small animals that would hide in the rocks, shrubs and trees that grew up its flanks. Our hearts were always filled with terror, though, when we heard the bark of a baboon. We knew that, even if we could only hear one barking, there would be a whole troop of them close by. Baboons are large, very strong animals. Males can weigh up to 49 kilograms. They have long, sharp teeth and can cause a lot of damage. They are not cute, like monkeys, and they seem quite mean-spirited.

A farmer once told me that a troop of baboons lived on the mountainside alongside his farm. They particularly liked his kitchen garden, and during the late afternoon they would come down like an army and take charge of the vegetable patch. They ate the lettuce, the cabbage and the cauliflower. They loved the juicy red tomatoes and tore away the runner beans from their vines. Most of all, though, they loved the pumpkin seeds inside the pumpkins. Pumpkin skins are hard to break. They would use stones to make a small hole in them, just enough to push one small fist through, and they'd pull out the seeds to eat. The farmer grew quite desperate. Other farmers shot at the marauding baboons, but my friend knew there would be no wild animals left in the country if everyone did that, so he tried to protect his produce as best he could.

One morning he walked through his vegetable patch to check that everything was growing well. When he got to the bed where the pumpkins grew, he was quite shocked to find a young baboon lying on the ground, looking quite desperate, with a huge, round pumpkin attached to his hand. The young baboon had not obeyed the baboon law, which is to always stay together. While the rest of the baboons were sleeping, he had quietly crept off to the vegetable patch to have a feast all by himself. He had grabbed at the seeds. There were so many in his hand that it got stuck. Of course, if he had let go of the seeds, he could have easily slipped his hand out. He was not a self-controlled, disciplined baboon at all, and he wasn't willing to let go of the seeds. Sadly, he had trapped himself in a pumpkin and had lost his freedom. How sad!

Sometimes we are like that baboon. We get trapped through our own choices, and don't know how to break free from the silly things that become important to us.

Self-control? Self-discipline? A baboon would never know what they were; but I am sure you know how important they are for living well!

PRAYER

When I am tempted to do what I feel like doing without any thought or self-control, help me to do what is right and good. Amen.

Camels – 'The Ships of the Desert'

THEME

God gives us the resources to get through difficulties and to resist temptation.

BIBLE GEM

'My grace is sufficient for you, for my power is made perfect in weakness.' *2 Corinthians 12:9*

YOU COULD USE

- A soft toy camel
- A carved wooden camel or train of camels – easy to find in charity shops

ILLUSTRATION

Whenever I see a camel, I think of the wise men riding on them from the East with their gifts to welcome Jesus after His birth. The camel is quite an extraordinary animal that people have used to work for them for five thousand years. People still use them today to plough fields and to transport goods, as they have always done.

Camels are large animals and measure up to seven feet tall. They are strong, heavy beasts and weigh anything between six hundred and fifty pounds (295kg) and one thousand, three hundred pounds (590kg). They have long, strong legs, and they can use all four of them to kick! Their feet are wide, tough and thickly padded so that they will not be fazed by walking on the hot desert sand.

One of the most obvious features of the camel is the hump on its back. Dromedaries only have one hump. When there is plenty of food, camels will store the food they don't use as fat in their humps. When they travel through the desert and there is little or no food to eat, the fat in their humps will be used to feed and water them. Camels can go for several weeks without food or water. Their humps shrink gradually as they use up the fat stores in them.

When they do reach an oasis, they can gulp down 181 litres of water at once in less than three minutes (which means that when Rebekah watered Abraham's servant's camels she managed quite a feat!).

The camel has several other features that help it to withstand the harsh conditions of the desert. For instance, did you know that the thick fur on its hump and head protects it from the sun where it can be as hot as 65°C? The fur reflects the sun, so it doesn't feel as warm. The fur also helps it to stay warm in the winter on the cold desert nights.

Did you know that the camel has three sets of eyelids that it uses to protect its eyes from damage by the sand in the sandstorms? One of the sets of eyelids works like safety glasses. They are very thin and allow the camel to see through them, but stop the sand and dust blowing into them. Its double row of eyelashes also helps to protect its eyes in the sandstorms.

The camel's lips are especially thick so that it will not feel pain when it eats thorns and cactuses growing in the desert. Its lips are split and can work separately, helping it to pick up food.

Isn't it impressive how well equipped the camel is to survive in the desert? Without its hump, its special eyelids and eyelashes, its interesting lips and special fur, it would not survive.

Sometimes life can be harsh for us, too. Sometimes people make it hard for us to be followers of Jesus. They think we are weird. In those times we need to be just as prepared and resourceful as the camel to survive. Our text tells us that God's grace is all we need. When we recognise how weak we are, God gives us all the strength we need to get through.

PRAYER

Father God, please give me all the resources I need to be true to You today. Amen.

Donkeys Aren't Dumb!

sermon 4

THEME

It is wise to say only positive things about our friends, our families and our church.

BIBLE GEM

'The words of the reckless pierce like swords, but the tongue of the wise brings healing.'
Proverbs 12:18

YOU COULD USE

- Make a donkey puppet by gluing a donkey face onto a paper bag; use your hand to make it speak.
- Alternatively, there are very cheap animal masks in toy shops, in party shops and on the internet. Wear the mask yourself when you tell the story of Balaam.

ILLUSTRATION

[Make the braying sound of a donkey first. Don't let the children see the puppet or mask at this stage.] Do you know which animal makes that sound? [Let the children respond.] There are several times when donkeys are mentioned in the Bible. Donkeys have been used to carry loads, or people, and to pull carts, for thousands of years.

Did you know that they can hear very well? They can hear the bray of a donkey as far as ninety-six kilometres away in the desert!

Donkeys are social animals and like living in herds. They can remember places they have visited and other donkeys they may not have seen for a long time. Their memories are good.

They are always on the lookout for danger, and if they sense any, they absolutely avoid it. Curiously, they are not as stubborn as people describe them. They are actually intelligent about sensing danger.

This reminds me of a story in Numbers 22: Balak, the King of the Moabites, was jittery. He had noticed how the Israelites seemed to win every battle with his neighbours, and he didn't want to lose in a battle with them. Balak believed in the power of evil spirits and curses. He sent his men to Balaam and asked him to go with them to the Israelite camp to curse them. They offered to pay him.

At first, Balaam refused the money and said he needed to ask God about it. God told him not to go with the men, not to take the money and not to say anything bad about the Israelites.

Balak asked again, offering more money. When Balaam asked God what he should do, God told him to agree to go with the men to the camp. "Yes!" Balak smiled, "Balaam will curse them, and they won't be a threat to us ever." He cheered.

Balaam and his donkey had hardly started their journey when the donkey ran off the road in fright. Balaam was annoyed, and he beat it furiously. He could not see the angel in the middle of the road, blocking the donkey.

They tried again. The angel returned. As the donkey veered to the edge, Balaam grazed his foot against the stone wall. He was furious, and beat the donkey even harder this time.

Again, at the narrowest place in the road, the angel appeared and held out a sword. This time the donkey sat down and refused to budge. Balaam was about to beat it again when the donkey spoke: "What have I done to make you beat me three times?"

The angel asked Balaam, "Why are you beating that donkey when it saved your life three times? I would have killed you if it hadn't stopped." Now Balaam understood that it was God speaking through the donkey. God had sent an angel to stop him in his tracks, and he promised to do whatever God asked.

When they reached the camp there was blessing, not cursing. The lesson Balaam learned is good for us too: to speak well of our friends, our families, our pastor and the members in our church.

PRAYER

Dear Jesus, help me to be wise with my words and only ever to speak well of others. Amen.

The Chameleon (5)

THEME

Be on your guard. Don't allow yourself to be misled!

BIBLE GEM

'Jesus answered: "Watch out that no-one deceives you." ' *Matthew 24:4*

YOU COULD USE

- A stuffed or plastic toy chameleon
- A collection of different toy chameleons

ILLUSTRATION

Tell me . . . do you know which creature has been called the 'master of disguise'? This is because it can change colour to blend into the surroundings without drawing attention to itself: a chameleon, of course! I remember picking green chameleons off my mother's rose shrubs when I was young. I also remember when a boy in my class at school picked up a brown one from some tall dried grass. He put it on his shoulder. It nipped him on the ear, and it bled a lot. He wasn't happy!

Chameleons belong to the lizard family, and there are one hundred and sixty species of them in the world. Their natural habitats are in Africa, Southern Europe, South Asia and Sri Lanka. Wonderful things happen in the cells called chromatophores, just below the outer layer of their skin. The top layer has yellow and red pigments, and the lower layer has blue and white ones. When the brain sends a message to the cells to get bigger or smaller, the pigments in the cells mix, and the colours spread along the melanin fibres. They have an inbuilt colour wheel or make-up palette – this is how they can change colour in 20 seconds.

Chameleons don't just change colour to blend in with their surroundings, but also to reflect the mood they are in, or to make themselves feel more comfortable, or to communicate with other chameleons.

The other interesting feature is that they have 360-degree vision because their eyes can swivel 360 degrees. They can see in two directions at the same time.

Chameleons range in size from about fifteen millimetres long to sixty-eight and a half centimetres.

They have amazing tongues which they use to catch their prey. One and a half to twice the length of their bodies, their tongues can reach their prey in 0.07 seconds.

Chameleons' feet are shaped more like tongs, and this helps them to grip onto thin or rough branches.

When I think of the disguised chameleon blending into the vegetation so it is barely noticeable, and I think of its tongue that shoots out like a bullet to grab its prey, I am reminded of a story in the Bible where a serpent disguised itself in a tree and charmed Eve to taste the fruit of the tree of knowledge of good and evil. He deceived her, telling her that she would be wise if she ate it. She believed him, and discovered that she had made a terrible choice by believing that lie. It is so easy for us to be deceived by others. Jesus warns us to watch out! Don't be deceived. There will be people who will tell you all kinds of lies in His name. Know Jesus, study His word and stay close to Him, and you will be safe.

PRAYER

Father, God, thank You for warning us about the dangers of blending in, of being deceived. Keep us close to Your heart, today and every day. Amen.

Meerkats

sermon 6

THEME

We are stronger when we work together.

BIBLE GEM

'Live in harmony with one another.' *Romans 12:16*

YOU COULD USE

- A soft toy meerkat; and/or
- You could cut out an enlarged photograph of the meerkat and glue it to a lolly stick to make a puppet.
- Photographs of meerkats can be found in books and downloaded from the internet.

ILLUSTRATION

Here is Mervyn Meerkat. He's a friendly little chap. Would you like to say hello to him? It is unusual for Mervyn to be on his own. He lives with his family, known as a mob or gang, of around thirty meerkats. His family are important to him. He looks after them, and they look after him.

The meerkat family live in intricate burrows and channels underground in the desert areas of Southern Africa. They have large eyes and pointy little noses. Meerkat mobs are known for the way they work together and support each other. They do everything together, such as hunting, eating, taking care of each other's babies, teaching the babies how to be good, successful meerkats, and protecting each other.

They are alert, and are often seen standing on their hind legs, on the lookout for any danger, such as snakes, birds of prey and jackals (related to a fox), who eat them. Whenever they sense danger, they jump up and down, barking and hissing to put off their predators and drive them off.

When the meerkat family are busy with all their duties in the burrow, a single meerkat will stand on sentry duty outside the burrow. He will find the highest point of the burrow and will keep guard dutifully for about two hours. While on duty, he will not sneak off for a snack or drink, no matter how hungry or thirsty he may be. He will wait at his spot until the next meerkat turns up to take his place and do the next shift.

These wonderful little creatures, though very sociable and such good team players, are fierce fighters and will fight to the death to protect the rest of the meerkats in the mob.

They remind us that we each have our own part to play in our families by working together for the good of everyone. Do we grumble about our chores, thinking they are unfair? What if we thought about doing our chores faithfully, knowing that it is a help to everyone in the family? Do we do our best to make everyone in the family happy? Do we do little favours for each other just because we want to?

Let Mervyn Meerkat remind you that our families are strongest when they work together in love. . . .

PRAYER

Dear Jesus, I want to play my part and live in harmony
with my family. Thank You for promising to help me. Amen.

A Sad Tale of a Greedy Squirrel

sermon

(7)

THEME

Greed is one of the deadly sins.

BIBLE GEM

'What good is it for someone to gain the whole world, yet forfeit their soul?' *Mark 8:36*

YOU COULD USE

- Bird feeders – particularly the plastic tube variety
- Some plant bulbs

ILLUSTRATION

Some people find squirrels funny and cute – I guess they are, but they really do annoy me a lot! Let me tell you why. . . .

Not a day goes by without a few pesky squirrels visiting my garden and getting up to all kinds of mischief. They are greedy creatures, always on the lookout for food; and they don't mind breaking things and destroying things to get what they want! Sometimes they appear to break things just for the fun of it.

Last autumn, I planted loads of snowdrops, daffodils and tulips. I knew that we would welcome their jewel-like colours after a long, grey winter. The squirrels had different ideas, though. They thought it was party time, and they were determined to have a feast. In three days, they managed to dig up and chew all the snowdrops. It seems that tulips are like cake to them, because they dug those up, too. There was soil everywhere; some half-chewed bulbs lay scattered on the lawn, on the patio and in the flower beds. It left me furious and discouraged! The garden nurseries had sold out of the bulbs I wanted, and I just had to buy the last few bulbs that nobody wanted. I planted them anyway, and my husband made some covers to protect the bulbs so that the squirrels couldn't dig them up.

And then the winter came. It was a very long, cold one, and I put out the bird feeders to help them through it. The squirrels were there again, scaring the birds so they could steal their food. (We have bought every kind of bird feeder that claims to be squirrel-proof. Believe me, there aren't any.) Nothing – no obstacle or trick one can think of – will deter a squirrel from finding a way to those precious nuts and seeds!

In a very icy week, none of us ventured out into the garden: but one of the squirrels did. One managed to knock down one of the plastic tube feeders and pulled off the lid. Greedily, he feasted and ate his way into the tube. His greed got the better of him, because he ate so much that he got stuck in the cylinder and was unable to get out, and that was the end of him. We only noticed it when the weather had improved a bit.

I hoped that the other squirrels had noticed and learned a lesson, but I'm afraid they still chew off the tender little rose buds on my bushes and dig out plants from their pots. But I learned the lesson they should have. Jesus told a crowd of people to watch that they are not overcome by greed. When greed overtakes us, we want more than we have, more than we need. Jesus asked His listeners what the point was of trying to get more than we need while forgetting that it is God who gives us everything we need.

Every time I see a bird feeder, I am reminded of that greedy little fellow and the good advice Jesus gave us. It is said that greed is one of the deadly sins. If the squirrel family who visit my garden could speak, they would probably agree!

PRAYER

Dear Jesus, everything You did came from a loving, generous heart: never from greed. Remove every hint of greed from my heart now. Amen.

The Elephants' Ancient Pathways

THEME

Jesus is the way to eternal life.

BIBLE GEM

'Jesus answered, "I am the way and the truth and the life. No-one comes to the Father except through me." ' *John 14:6*

YOU COULD USE

- A toy elephant
- Enlarged photographs of elephants

ILLUSTRATION

How many of you have seen a real elephant? Was it in a zoo? In a game park? What are the first things you notice about the African elephant?

African elephants have enormous ears. Do you think they help them to hear better? It is true that they do, but they also use them as big fans to cool themselves in the hot African sun. Did you know that they also listen through their feet? When elephants become conscious of a predator or nearby danger, they stomp their feet to warn any other elephants who may be in the vicinity. Those elephants pick up the vibrations in the ground through the nerves in the pads under their feet.

The first thing I notice about an elephant is its long trunk. Trunks are unusual because they are the joining of the top lip and the nose. Elephants breathe and smell through their trunks. Did you know that they can smell water from several miles away? They also use them to make sounds. We say that elephants 'trumpet'. They use their trunks for feeling, holding onto and picking up things. Can your nose do all those things? Do you know how many muscles humans have in their bodies? [639.] Elephants have over 40,000 muscles in their trunks alone. They can lift things that weigh just over 700 lbs!

Some years ago, people across the world were worried that too many elephants were being killed. Scientists worked hard to find ways to protect them. They tracked them to study their behaviour to help find the best solution. They had known all along that elephants had great memories, and that they knew where the watering holes were, but they learned that the elephants actually followed the ancient pathways of their grandparents, great-grandparents, and great-great-grandparents. The traditional pathways for the Southern African elephants went through Angola up to Central Africa. Their pathway on the Angola border had been blocked by electric fences in the civil war. When they reached the fences they were anxious, frustrated and very sad. Their brains knew where to go, but the fences were a barrier. The scientists believe that their knowledge of these ancient watering holes is passed on from the oldest female elephant in the herd, known as the 'matriarch'. Her role is to lead the herd to the watering holes while the rest follow and show her enormous respect. The herd know that their lives depend on her knowledge and guidance.

The scientists were able to get governments to open spaces for the elephants to walk on their ancient pathways again. At last, the elephants were able to follow the pathways of their ancestors.

Most African elephants need to drink the equivalent of a bath filled with water. No wonder they have left well-trodden paths to their watering holes! Jesus tells us that He is the pathway to truth and life: no other path will take us to where we need to be. He has cleared away all the barriers.

PRAYER

Dear Jesus, thank You for being the pathway that will lead me to know You and to be with You forever. Amen.

An Amazing Friendship of the Unlikeliest of Animals

sermon 9

THEME

Heaven will be a peaceful, happy place.

BIBLE GEM

'The wolf will live with the lamb, the leopard will lie down with the goat, the calf and the lion and the yearling together; and a little child will lead them.' *Isaiah 11:6*

YOU WILL NEED

- Toy or wooden carved hippos and tortoises.

ILLUSTRATION

Their feet sank into the warm, soft white sand as they walked along the Mombasa beach that Boxing Day morning. Quiet and still, there was little sign of what was to come. Suddenly, Paula and her son, Joshua, noticed that the sea had become menacing and threatening, surging beyond its normal limit and way above the high-water mark. The tsunami which had started in Banda Aceh, Indonesia, twelve hours before had travelled 4,000 miles and had now reached the coast in East Africa.

Grabbing each other by the hand, they dashed back home to crying relatives who couldn't get over the devastating images they had seen on their televisions in the wake of the tsunami in the Indian Ocean. Paula and Joshua were fortunate. They had not come to harm.

However, about 40 miles from their home near Malindi, a family of hippos had been washed out to sea in a heavy storm a few days earlier. The people had struggled to coax the hippos back up the estuary, but now the tsunami had complicated the rescue even more. All but one of the hippos, it seemed, had disappeared. It was the baby! Stranded and forlorn, they saw him out on the reef. Hundreds of people tried to rescue him, using anything they thought may help. Ropes, boats, fishing nets, cars – nothing seemed to work. At last a brave young man lunged at the baby hippo and caught him.

Paula agreed to give the hippo sanctuary. She was asked to collect him in Malindi and to bring him to Mombasa. By now the hippo had been given a name, Owen, after the brave young man who had caught him.

Owen was very confused when he was released in Haller Park, his new home. He immediately ran up to a 130-year-old giant tortoise, called Mzee, whom he adopted as his mother. These two unlikeliest of animals became inseparable. I was fascinated by this story when it was reported on the BBC news in 2005. Can you imagine how delighted I was to see the affection these two amazing creatures had for each other when I visited Mombasa in 2006?

Unusual pairings like these do not happen very often in nature because dangers lurk all around. Isaiah has promised that that is how things will be in heaven: the hunted and the hunters will be friends; no animal or human will be fearful of anything. Heaven will be a safe, peaceful place where we can trust each other completely. Isaiah did not say that the hippo would lie with the giant tortoise, but he could have, because he used other unlikely examples, like the lamb and the lion, and the leopard and the goat.

I can just imagine seeing a giant tortoise mothering a baby hippo again in heaven! Won't that be amazing?

PRAYER

Dear Jesus, You have promised that heaven will be a safe, wonderful place where we can all get on together and live in peace. Help me to be at peace with everyone I know. Amen.

Bear, the Faithful Dog

THEME

Friends are loyal to each other whether times are good or bad.

BIBLE GEM

'We are still alive because the LORD's faithful love never ends. Every morning he shows it in new ways! You are so very true and loyal! I say to myself, "The LORD is my God, and I trust him." '
Lamentations 3:22-24 (ERV)

YOU COULD USE

- A real dog – make sure it is a gentle animal, used to children, and hold it as you speak to them; or
- A soft toy dog

ILLUSTRATION

How many of you have a pet dog at home? What is special about your dog? How do you look after it? Have you heard of the expression, 'A dog is man's best friend'? Do you think that is true? There are good reasons why dogs are called 'man's best friend'. They make good friends because they are protective and intensely loyal to their owner's family.

Have you watched a guide dog help a sight-impaired person walking through town or onto the bus or train? It is humbling to see an animal take such great care of a human being! Guide dogs are trained from birth for eighteen months to help those who cannot see. In the first twelve months they are house-trained and go through obedience training. If that goes well, they are trained for another six months in intelligent disobedience – that is, knowing when to disobey their handler because of dangers they can see that the blind person cannot. They are also trained to judge the height and width of spaces so that the blind person will not be in danger of tripping or bumping into things. Finally, the dog and the blind person train together for two weeks before they set off on their working partnership.

I recently read a story about a family who were caught up in the fires in Northern California. The family woke up to huge flames raging close to their home. There was no time to spare, and they fled immediately. Their dog panicked and disappeared into the smoke.

It upset them to think about what might have happened to him. Two days later, they couldn't bear it any more, and they made their way through the smouldering ashes of their home.

'Bear!' they called repeatedly. Nothing!

'Bear, Bear, where are you?' they kept calling.

And then, past the gate and where the house once stood (but now burnt to the ground), someone saw Bear!

The Bernese mountain dog jumped up, placed his paws on their shoulders, wagged his tail vigorously, and licked their faces.

Patiently waiting for his family, Bear could only do what faithful, loyal friends do – he would be there waiting for them in the tough times, too!

Our Bible text reminds us that Jesus remains loyal to us, even when we are not loyal to Him. So often we are fair-weather friends, and the friendship lasts only so long as it is convenient. Jesus says He will love us and be loyal to us forever. Will you promise to be loyal to Him too?

PRAYER

Dear Jesus, thank You for being loyal to me through thick and thin. Help me to be loyal to my family, to my friends and especially to You! Amen.

Bats Aren't Batty!

sermon **11**

THEME
I choose to live peacefully with my neighbours.

BIBLE GEM
'Seek the Lord while you can find him. Call upon him now while he is near.' *Isaiah 55:6 (TLB)*

YOU COULD USE
- Toy bats
- Enlarged photographs of bats

ILLUSTRATION

Unfortunately, made-up stories and horror films have given many the wrong impression of bats. They are not the evil, frightening creatures that some think they are. In fact, they are important for our ecosystem. Maybe we can find out why in the next few minutes. Did you know that there are 2,277 species of bats, which make up about 40% of all mammal species on earth? That represents a lot of creatures that we barely ever see! The megabats have good eyesight and feed on fruit and nectar. Microbats, on the other hand, do not rely on their sight, but on echolocation, to go where they want to go. Have you ever been in a place where you have heard your own echo? Echolocation works in a similar way: the bat makes high-pitched sounds, which are so high that only other bats can hear them. When those sound waves reach the insect or the other bat, or even a human, the interrupted wave echoes back. This helps the bat to have a very accurate idea of the space and how it is filled around it. Their ability to locate through echoes is so great, they can even sense a single strand of hair!

As bats are constantly relying on echolocation in their flight, it reminds me of the text in 1 Chronicles 16:11 where we are encouraged to seek the Lord and His strength continually. We also can echolocate spiritually through prayer, and by staying close to Jesus.

Here are some other interesting facts about bats: they are the best pest-controllers around, and the good thing about them is that they do not poison the environment as pest-control sprays do! Did you know that some bats can eat more than 600 flying insects per hour?

Another interesting fact is that they prefer a vegetarian diet. Most of them like fruit, pollen and nectar, and insects of course. Only a very small number of the microbats drink blood.

Something else that is so unusual about them is that their circulatory systems work in the opposite way to ours. This is because they hang upside down for long periods at a time. This helps the blood to flow easily to every part of their body when they are upside down.

They appear to have wings, but they are webbed fingers, making them the only mammals that can fly.

Another interesting fact about bats is that they often share their homes with thousands of other bats. Apparently, the largest natural bat colony is the Bracken Bat Cave in Texas. Can you believe that twenty million bats live there together? When they leave the cave together at the same time, they rise in the sky like a dark cloud that can be seen for miles.

Isn't it extraordinary to think of bats allowing other bats to share their space with them? As children of God we have been encouraged to 'share [our] belongings with [our] needy fellow-Christians' (Romans 12:13, GNB). If bats can do you it, surely we can, too.

PRAYER

Loving Father, You made the tiniest bat and gave it such amazing abilities. Help me to turn to You every day and to live peacefully with my neighbours. Amen.

A Hungry Arctic Fox

THEME

Jesus promised to fill those who hunger for Him.

BIBLE GEM

'Blessed are those who hunger and thirst for righteousness, for they will be filled.' *Matthew 5:6*

YOU COULD USE

- Toys or pictures of the Arctic fox

ILLUSTRATION

If you like dogs and watching how they behave, you'll probably find the Arctic fox just as fascinating, because it is related to dogs and other foxes. Arctic foxes are the smallest of the foxes, about the same size as a domestic cat. They live in the tundra and pack-ice regions of the Arctic circle, where temperatures are very cold. They can live in these harsh, icy conditions (up to -70 degrees Celsius) thanks to their thick fur, which insulates them from the cold, keeping their body temperature constant. Even their feet are furry. They are said to have the warmest fur of any Arctic animal, even more than the polar bear.

Like swans, they mate for life, and both Mummy and Daddy Fox take care of the pups as they grow up. Apart from these 'family times', they tend to live on their own.

Most of their time is spent hunting for food. They use all their senses when they hunt. Their sense of hearing is so sensitive, they can even hear small rodents and creatures below ground. When they do, they will sit and wait until an animal pops up, and will then pounce on it for their meal. They will also follow in the tracks of polar bears and wait until they have finished eating their kill. When the polar bears have moved on, they will eat up the leftovers. They are happy to eat others' leftovers. People who have watched them say that this is when they display their playful, cheeky side, and that is why they are called the 'clowns of the tundra'.

There was an amazing report in July 2019 of a hungry Arctic fox who had walked from the Norwegian Svalbard islands all the way to Northern Canada. Scientists were able to track her because they had fitted her with a satellite tracking collar in March of the previous year. After they had released her, she went on her amazing journey. It took her three weeks to travel 940 miles to reach Greenland. Then she walked another 1,200 miles across the Greenland ice sheet and down to Ellesmere Island in Canada. The whole journey took her an impressive 76 days.

The scientists who tracked her believe she was looking for food. Isn't it amazing how motivating hunger can be? In the Sermon on the Mount, Jesus told His listeners that those who hunger after righteousness will be filled. They will not be left to starve. He has promised that those who follow Him because they want to be more like Him will be given that ability. I wonder: are we as hungry to be filled with the words of Jesus as that Arctic fox was for food?

PRAYER

Dear Jesus, help me to feast on Your Word and Your righteousness. Amen.

The Zebra  sermon 13

sermon 13

THEME

God uses several ways to protect us.

BIBLE GEM

'But the Lord is faithful, and he will strengthen you and protect you from the evil one.'
2 Thessalonians 3:3

YOU COULD USE

- A soft toy zebra or a plastic one
- Enlarged photographs of the three species of zebra: Burchell's zebra; Grevy's zebra; and Equus or mountain zebra
- Any artefact made from zebra pelts
- A scarf, shoes, or fabric with a zebra design

ILLUSTRATION

Zebras are stunningly beautiful creatures. Their black-and-white markings have inspired designers for centuries. [Show the children some of the artefacts and items you have.]

Did you know that there are only three species of zebra in the wild: Burchell's zebra, Grevy's zebra and the Equus zebra? Zebras are only found in Africa, and are part of the horse and donkey family. Unlike horses and donkeys, which have been tamed and trained to work for humans, zebras have never been tamed, because they are even more stubborn than donkeys!

Scientists have studied zebras for years, trying to work out why they have markings that make them stand out so much. They once thought that the stripes might be a good camouflage as they move through the shadows in the long grass, but they have since given up on that theory.

A group of scientists wondered if the stripes might protect them from flies and stinging insects, so they did research on it. They watched them very closely over several months, and discovered that, even though just as many flies and insects buzzed around the zebras as around the horses, the flies and insects did not land on the zebras, but they did land on the horses. They concluded that the stripes confused the insects. Maybe they made them dizzy, and this could be why they did not land on them. They also noticed that the zebras' tails were stronger and quicker at flicking the pests away. Maybe the scientists are still trying work out all the reasons there are for their beautiful stripes.

Each of the species of zebra has a different stripe pattern. Grevy zebras from Ethiopia have lots of narrow stripes, and the Burchell's zebras found in Southern Africa have much broader stripes. The Equus or mountain zebras from Angola and Namibia are somewhere in between. Even with these variations, did you know that no two zebras have the same stripes? You can always tell one apart from another by their stripes.

Zebras live in small family groups, but they like to get together with other family groups like a big church congregation or camp meeting! Even when they are in a big gathering, the families stay together.

Zebras seem to know that there is safety in staying together as a family and in mixing with other herding animals like antelopes.

Just as their stripes protect the zebras from stinging insects and annoying flies, and their family units and big gatherings protect them from danger, we are reminded that Jesus offers us protection from the dangers and temptations we face every day. He has given us loving, protective families and church families. He has given us His Word. Isn't He wonderful?

PRAYER

Dear Jesus, learning about the zebras and the way You designed them to keep them safe reminds us that You have promised to protect us from dangers and bad influences. Thank You for our families, for our pastor and for our friends at church. Amen.

Sheep

THEME

Jesus is my Shepherd, and He knows me. I must learn to recognise His voice.

BIBLE GEM

'Acknowledge that the LORD is God. He made us, and we belong to him; we are his people, we are his flock.' *Psalm 100:3 (GNB)*

YOU COULD USE

- A sheep soft toy
- Photographs of sheep
- If you can, bring in a live small lamb and hold it as you talk to the children.

ILLUSTRATION

Most people think that sheep are not very smart. Let me share some interesting facts about sheep with you, and you can make up your mind if you think they are smart or not.

Sheep have good memories. Those who have studied sheep closely say that they can remember at least fifty other sheep and people over a long period of time. In fact, the process and part of the brain that they use for this is similar to what humans use!

While people show how they feel by the expressions on their faces, such as smiling or frowning, sheep show how they feel by the way they move and position their ears. For example, if their ears face forward, they are either stressed or inquisitive. When their ears go back, they are usually fearful, and when their ears stand out straight to the side, they are calm. This is usually when they are feeding or being cuddled.

Sometimes, when they are frustrated, you will see them with one ear forward and the other backward. Scientists have noted that they change the position of their ears more when they are stressed. What is more, they can recognise emotion in us humans; and, apparently, they are more drawn to us when we smile!

They also make different sounds to each other to express how they feel.

When we are ill, we rely on a doctor to find out what is wrong with us and to prescribe the correct medicine to make us better. With some illnesses, sheep know what their problem is, and they also know which plants to look for and eat to make them better.

Sheep can see behind themselves without turning their heads. This is because their eyes can roll almost 300 degrees!

Sheep are sociable animals. They like being close together.

Ewes (mother sheep) take good care of their lambs. They keep a close eye on them all the time, and when they wander too far, they call them back. Each ewe has a special bleat that her baby lamb recognises immediately, and the lamb will run back to her immediately.

Sheep are smart? Not very smart? What do you think?

There are several stories in the Bible about sheep and shepherds. Jesus called Himself the Shepherd, and He called us the lambs of His flock. He told a story of the Good Shepherd who went to find the one lamb who had strayed away. He never gave up. When he had found it, he carried it back to the safety of the fold.

The way sheep behave reminds us that we are safer together, helping and encouraging one another; and, just as the lamb knows and hears its mother's voice and runs back to her when she calls, we must know and recognise Jesus' voice, too. When you hear Him call to be careful, to come to His safe side, will you come running, too?

PRAYER

Thank You for being my Shepherd. Keep me close to Your side. Amen.

The Silkworm

THEME

Jesus died to save us from our sins.

BIBLE GEM

'But God has shown us how much he loves us – it was while we were still sinners that Christ died for us!' *Romans 5:8 (GNB)*

YOU WILL NEED

- Pieces of silk fabric
- Garments made from silk
- Bring in a box of silkworms if you can, or show some photographs of them downloaded from the internet.

ILLUSTRATION

[Show the children the pieces of silk fabric or garments made from silk. Ask them to feel them and to describe what they feel. In what way does it feel different from the clothes they are wearing?]

Where do you think this fabric was first made?

Today, some of you are wearing shirts made from cotton, which comes from a plant; others are wearing trousers or dresses made from polyester, which is a man-made plastic material. Some of you are wearing cardigans or jumpers made from wool, which comes from sheep, goats or lamas. I wonder how many of us are wearing something made from silk. It is a very expensive fabric that the Chinese started making about 5,000 years ago. Actually, they didn't make the thread. They only worked out how to use the thread to weave into fabric. This expensive material is made by a worm: a silkworm! The worm makes one long strand of silk by secreting a protein from two salivary glands in its head. Each of those long, very thin strands could be anything between 300 and 900 metres long.

The Chinese learned that the silk thread cannot be used from the cocoons if the moth breaks free from it and leaves a hole. When it does this, the thread is cut into lots of short little threads that are useless. To avoid this, they throw the cocoons into boiling water as soon as they are formed to kill the pupae (the silkworms inside the cocoon) so they cannot break the thread. Then they unwind the silk.

The Chinese kept their knowledge of making silk thread and fabric secret for hundreds of years. Silk traders across Asia and Europe became very wealthy. Later, two monks managed to smuggle some silkworm eggs out of China, and today China, Japan, Italy, Spain and France produce silk cloth which is sold all around the world. Just imagine: it takes three thousand cocoons to produce five hundred grams of silk! Just imagine: five thousand silkworms sacrifice their cocoons to make just one kimono (famous Japanese traditional gown).

When I was young, like you, I used to keep silkworms in a shoebox with holes poked in the lid so they could breathe. I would feed them fresh green mulberry leaves every day. They chomped away at them for four to six weeks and grew longer and fatter. As soon as they were the right size, they would pupate and then take about three days to spin a cocoon. I cut out simple shapes from card and placed the worms on them, and they would spin their thread around the shapes. At the end I would have small pieces of soft, glistening raw silk. Some of the worms just span tight, bullet-shaped cocoons. About three weeks later, the moth would push its way from the bottom of the cocoon and then it would lay loads of tiny eggs, from which the next season's silkworms would hatch.

Isn't it amazing how the silkworm is sacrificed for the silk to be of any use? It reminds me of the sacrifice Jesus made by dying to save me. More than threads of pure silk, He has promised me that I can share His home in heaven with Him forever! And, do you know, He has promised the same for you!

PRAYER

Loving Jesus, thank You for promising me a place in heaven with You! Amen.

The Butterfly

THEME

Trials and challenges don't always do us harm. Through them we learn how to persevere.

BIBLE GEM

'Consider it pure joy . . . whenever you face trials of many kinds, because you know that the testing of your faith produces perseverance. Let perseverance finish its work so that you may be mature and complete, not lacking anything.'
James 1:2-4

YOU COULD USE

- Photographs and images of a butterfly and a cocoon
- Colourful plastic butterflies from garden centres

ILLUSTRATION

I love seeing butterflies flutter from flower to flower. Their colours and patterns and graceful movements are gentle and beautiful.

Do you know, butterflies didn't start life this way?

They started out as tiny, delicate little eggs; then they hatched out of those eggs as caterpillars, slowly moving from leaf to leaf, eating away at them until the time came when they started spinning cocoons for them to nestle into quietly. There, unnoticed, they began to transform into something quite extraordinary. Finally, the day arrived when a small opening appeared in each cocoon, and after several hours a butterfly forced its way through that small space and spread out its damp wings to dry.

I once heard a sad story about a man who sat on a bench and watched a butterfly trying to force its body through a tiny hole in the cocoon. It would wriggle and struggle for a bit; stop for a bit; and wriggle and struggle again. This went on for ages – and then it just stopped. Nothing happened, and it seemed it couldn't make any more progress. The man thought he could help it along. After all, butterflies are meant to fly free! He took out a small pair of scissors and opened the cocoon. The butterfly emerged easily, but sadly its body was withered, and its wings were all shrivelled.

The man expected the wings to open any minute before it would fly away, but the poor butterfly was deformed for life. It spent the rest of its days crawling because its wings weren't strong enough to fly.

The man had not realised that the butterfly needed to struggle to get through that tiny hole in the cocoon to force fluid from the body of the butterfly into its wings so that it would be ready to fly when it had broken free from the cocoon. The help he had given the butterfly had not been helpful after all.

It reminds me of a helpful text in the Bible from James 1:2-4 that tells us that we must be happy to face trials and challenges, because we learn to persevere when we try to overcome or master them. Have any of you had to struggle to master a skill, or to understand something you found difficult? Did you keep trying until you 'got it'? Isn't it wonderful that you not only mastered the swimming stroke, or difficult piece of music, or difficult words to spell, but also learned to persevere!

We will need to persevere and endure hardships many times throughout our lives. If we want to be successful, we may as well learn to persevere when we are young!

PRAYER

Dear Father God, thank You for giving me intellect and a will to try and try and try again. Like the butterfly, help me not to go for the easy option, but to learn the value of perseverance. Amen.

The Ant

sermon 17

THEME

Teamwork and industry are a blessing to everyone in the community.

BIBLE GEM

'Go to the ant, you sluggard; consider its ways and be wise.' *Proverbs 6:6*

YOU COULD USE

- A plastic toy ant (cheap to find at toy shops and the children's section in garden centres)
- A poster with '10,000,000,000,000,000' printed on it
- An enlarged photograph of an ant

ILLUSTRATION

I wonder if you can guess what I am. I'll give you some clues. . . .

- I am just one of 10 quadrillion of my kind who live on earth. That number is 10,000,000,000,000,000 (one with 16 zeros at the end of it!)[show the poster and compare it with the current world population, which is 7 billion];
- You can find my kind on every continent in the world except the Antarctic and Arctic regions;
- There are over 12,000 different species of my kind;
- The total mass of all my kind in the world is the same as or greater than the total mass of all humans living in the world;
- Our kind and humans are the only creatures who farm other creatures;
- I can lift objects three times my weight, and I can push up an object one hundred times my weight while hanging upside down;
- I am one of the world's strongest creatures relative to my size;

- Some of my kind live for just a few weeks, while others can live up to thirty years!
- I work for a queen!
- My kind live in colonies;
- Our largest colony discovered so far was in Southern Europe and was over 6,000km wide;
- Scientists have estimated that my kind move about fifty tons of soil every year in one square mile;
- One species of my kind is the most venomous insect in the world.

Yes, I am an ant!

Many years ago, Solomon, a very learned man, advised his son to watch the ants, to study them and to draw lessons from them. What strikes you most about them is that they are always busy, always going somewhere, always doing something, never giving up! They are never lazy!

It is wonderful how all their effort is for the good of the whole colony, not just for themselves. For example, they keep the nest warm by going for a walk in the sun, storing the warmth and then releasing the heat once they are back in the nest. They have two stomachs: one to feed themselves, and one to feed others. They take care of their nest by keeping the tunnels and rooms clean and tidy, and add to them by building more. They get rid of the rubbish by taking it out of the nest.

Are we as hard-working in our church family? Do we think of others before ourselves? Do we care for each other? Do we make our church a special, caring place where everyone feels loved and welcome? How can you be like the amazing ant?

PRAYER

Dear Father, thank You for creating the tiniest ant with such amazing ability and sense of family and teamwork. Help me to be just as helpful and hardworking at home and at church. Amen.

The Honeybee

THEME

Everyone in our church has an important part to play.

BIBLE GEM

'How good and pleasant it is when God's people live together in unity!' *Psalm 133:1*

YOU COULD USE

- A toy bee
- Finger-puppet bees made from black and yellow pipe cleaners and small wobbly eyes on your fingers as you talk to the children

ILLUSTRATION

[Keep the bee or finger-puppet bees behind your back when you start.]

Buzz, buzz, buzz! What is that buzzing sound? Where is all that noise coming from? [Now reveal the bees.]

Wow! These are busy bees. . . . Let me tell you about these busy bees and what they have been up to recently!

Yesterday each of these bees made ten trips, and each of them visited four hundred flowers. Did you know that they had to visit 4,200 flowers just to make one tablespoon of honey? Do you know, I didn't hear one of them complain that it was too hard, or that they were tired, or that the effort wasn't worth it. They just buzzed away and did what God made them to do.

Honeybees have double the number of receptors in the brain that help them to smell. They use these to communicate with each other in the hive, and for finding food. They are able to tell hundreds of different flowers apart from several metres, and whether they are good for pollinating or gathering nectar.

The buzzing sound bees make comes from their rapid wing stroke, which is about 200 beats per second. Bees can fly for six miles without stopping, and up to 15 miles per hour.

The average worker bee produces only about one twelfth of a teaspoon of honey in her lifetime.

A hive of bees will fly 90,000 miles, the equivalent of three orbits around the earth, to collect 1kg of honey.

A honeybee visits 50 to 100 flowers during a collection trip.

A colony of bees consists of 20,000-60,000 honeybees and one queen. Worker bees live for about six weeks and do all the work. The queen bee can live up to five years, and her role is to fill the hive with eggs. She is very busy in the summer, when the hive needs to be at its maximum strength: she lays up to 2,500 eggs per day. The drones fertilise the eggs and feed the larvae. No bee is more important than another, because the hive would die if they stopped doing what they do.

Each honeybee colony has a unique odour, which works like a password or security code.

The Bible tells us that our church family is like a healthy beehive: everyone has an important part to play in the church, and no one is more important than another. When you smile at that church member, when you join in the singing and prayers, you are bringing joy to everyone around you.

One of the reasons beehives work so well is that the bees communicate well with each other and they work hard to serve and support each other. When they find a good source of pollen, they share the good news with their bee companions, and they gather the nectar together.

At home, at school and at church, God calls you to be just as hardworking and faithful, and to serve others as willingly, as the bee. If we all did, can you imagine what God could do through us and through our church? Isn't that an exciting thought? Let's start right here, today, to live together and to work in unity! Let's keep the hive healthy . . . !

PRAYER

Dear Jesus, help me to be a good team player as I work for You. Bless my church family and make it grow big and strong for You! Amen.

Amazing Honey (19)

THEME

Kind words bring healing to others.

BIBLE GEM

'Gracious words are a honeycomb, sweet to the soul and healing to the bones.' *Proverbs 16:24*

YOU COULD USE

- A jar of honey with honeycomb in it
- Some vinegar in a small bowl

ILLUSTRATION

I had some delicious honey on my toast this morning! Do you know how to make honey? Can we make honey, like jam perhaps? Of course not! Only bees can make honey! Unlike jam, which isn't that good for you, honey is quite amazing. Did you know that bees are the only insects that make food that we eat?

How do bees make the honey? First, they make the honeycomb, which is made up of small hexagonal waxy storage cells. To make just one pound of wax, they must eat six to eight pounds of honey. During the winter, they feed on the honey they produced in the warm summer months. They stay close together to keep the queen and themselves warm.

When I was a child, my mother used to remind me 'to sweeten my words with honey, not vinegar'. By that she encouraged me to speak kindly to others, and not to hurt them with harsh or cutting words. Honey is sweet, we know, and vinegar is very sour and acidic. It can even knock your breath away if you breathe in the vapour from it! Just look at someone screw up their face when they dip their finger in the vinegar and taste it. It isn't a nice experience at all.

Apart from its lovely flavour, honey has many other uses and benefits too. For example, did you know that it is the only food that includes all the vitamins, minerals and enzymes we need to stay alive? Not only that, but it also has an antioxidant that improves brain function and works like a medicine for so many illnesses and conditions. Here are just a few of them:

It is good for people who suffer with arthritic joints;

It is good for fighting colds;

It is good for stomach ulcers;

It is good for allergies like hay fever;

It is good for sleeplessness;

It is good for poor digestion;

It is good as a facial cleanser and hair conditioner;

It is good as a cough mixture;

It works like an antiseptic on wounds, bites and stings;

It has natural antibiotics to fight microbial infections;

Many hospitals use honey dressings for wound treatments and burns.

Could sweetening our words with honey also bring healing to others, as honey does to our bodies? The person you are talking to may not be physically ill, but they may be hurting in other ways. Maybe they are going through a rough patch; maybe they are troubled about something or have problems that seem impossible to solve. Your honey-sweetened words to them could bring them the encouragement they need to push on, to work things out and to leave what they must to God. Your words could help them to know that they are loved.

What do you think words of vinegar might sound like? Would they be harsh, unkind, critical, unhelpful, discouraging, judgemental, condemning? What about the tone of voice when those words are spoken? Would they be painful to hear?

It reminds me of the story of Jesus when He spoke gently to Zacchaeus as he sat up in the tree. His words were sweetened with honey, and they changed Zacchaeus's heart forever. He stopped cheating the people, paid them back everything that he owed, and more. I often wonder: if Jesus had spoken words of vinegar, would he have had the same change of heart?

Just as the bees spend their entire lives creating an atmosphere of sweetness and pleasantness, and just as Jesus sweetened His words with honey, will you do the same? It takes courage and discipline not to lash out with angry and stinging words sometimes, but it makes such a difference to the person you are talking to if you don't. It makes you a stronger, braver person, too!

PRAYER

Dear Jesus, may the words from my mouth be kind and healing as honey from the honeycomb. Amen.

The Trapdoor Spider

sermon 20

sermon 20

THEME

We are safe in God's protective care.

BIBLE GEM

'You are my hiding-place; you will protect me from trouble and surround me with songs of deliverance.'
Psalm 32:7

YOU COULD USE

- A jack-in-the-box (if you have one) or a small carton box with the bottom removed for your hand to go through and the top flap closed but free to open
- A spider puppet (if you have one) or one made from a black glove and two eyes stuck on it; use your thumb and forefinger to behave like forelegs

ILLUSTRATION

There is a wonderful little creature that lives in the nest it has burrowed about five inches underground. To keep it safe from predators, it has built a trapdoor which it keeps tightly shut so it will not be noticed. To further camouflage it, it covers the door with silk, earth, grass or moss. There are little holes inside the trapdoor which this creature holds onto to keep the door firmly shut if another creature tries to open it.

Shall we see what this creature is?

Wow! A spider. Meet Terry the trapdoor spider! Did you know that different types of trapdoor spiders are found all around the world, but their trapdoors do such a good job that we rarely see them!

Trapdoor spiders are meat eaters. They eat small insects which they must hunt or catch. Some spiders are adventurous and look for their prey close to their burrow. In the dark of night, others lift the door while stretching out their front legs. They wait patiently for the creature to come close to their legs. The hairs on their legs catch the vibrations and they grab them as soon as they are close. They return to the burrow nest, and the trapdoor slams shut.

The lifespan of a trapdoor spider is about five-to-twenty years, but the oldest known trapdoor spider, known as No. 16, was forty-three years old when it died. It lived in its burrow in a garden in Perth, Australia. It didn't die from old age, but from a wasp sting!

The lengths trapdoor spiders will go to to protect themselves are astonishing. Their efforts are rewarded, because they appear to have such good lifespans.

Just like the trapdoor spider, we would do well to protect ourselves from the influences around us that could draw us away from the safe arms of Jesus our Saviour.

Can you think what some of them may be?

Stay close to Jesus, today and every day . . .

PRAYER

Dear Jesus, keep me safe in Your care today. Amen.

The Spider's Web (sermon 21)

THEME

Don't get trapped by bad influences.

BIBLE GEM

'Do not be misled: "Bad company corrupts good character." ' *1 Corinthians 15:33*

YOU COULD USE

- A plastic spider's web from a children's toy shop
- A model of a spider's web made with several canes and twine

ILLUSTRATION

Did you know that spiders produce silk? You thought that only silkworms produced silk, didn't you? Spiders produce the silk to spin their webs, to make their egg sacs, and to tie up their prey.

The silk is stored in their bodies in a liquid form. When they want to make thread from it for their webs, they push it out through spinnerets (glands) on their abdomens. The thread comes out in lots of thin threads that stick together and harden in the air. Their webs look something like this. Starting in the middle, they spin the thread around in circles. [Show the children a model or a photograph of a web.] The spider uses these draglines to move quickly from one place to another. The difference between the silk from the silkworm and the spider's silk is that the spider's silk is sticky. The stickiness is not in the silk, but in a glue that it leaves on the threads. This glue is made from another gland in its body. This stickiness helps it to catch its prey. When its prey is caught, the spider either moves along a thread where the glue has not been added, or it uses small claws that prevent it from getting stuck in its own web. Scientists have tried several ways to use the spider's silk as we use the thread from the silkworm, but the sticky glue on it makes it impossible to use in the same way.

The spider's thread is extremely strong – it is said to be as strong as steel. It is also light and water-resistant, and can bend in the wind without breaking. Scientists have drawn on their knowledge of spider silk to design and make medical supplies that need the same qualities as those seen in the web. These have been designed to make stitches and glue to close wounds and bandages.

This past summer I was enjoying the sunshine and admiring some beautiful flowers growing in a pot on the patio. There was a large spider's web suspended between the flowers. That spider knew that insects would be attracted to the sparkling web when the sun shone on it. It also knew that they would be attracted to the beautiful flowers. I also admired the bees filling up their little pouches with pollen on some other flowers. Suddenly, one of the bees took off and flew straight into the web, got caught on one of the silk strands and battled to free herself from it. She got more and more desperate. I dashed into the house and collected a pair of scissors and quickly cut the thread the bee was attached to. She hesitated for a moment and then flew off. At that point, the spider dashed up one of the threads at lightning speed to where it expected the bee would be, only to find nothing there. Immediately, it started spinning again, creating a trap to lure another small insect.

There are lots of spider's webs that can trap us in life. The Bible reminds us to take care and not to be misled and become trapped in them. Bad company is a sure way to get trapped quickly and to be drawn away from Jesus.

PRAYER

Dear Jesus, give me eyes to see the danger around me and eyes that will only be attracted to You! Amen.

The Homing Pigeon

THEME

Jesus' followers are messengers of peace.

BIBLE GEM

'Let the peace of Christ rule in your hearts . . . and be thankful.' *Colossians 3:15*

YOU COULD USE

- Print out a large image of a pigeon on card.
- On a small, thin piece of paper, write the message: 'We are allies. Don't fire at us! Please rescue us!' Roll it up and tie it to the pigeon with thick cotton or thin string.

ILLUSTRATION

Pigeons and doves belong to the same bird family. There are several references to them in the Bible. Noah sent out a dove, probably knowing that it would come back, because doves and pigeons have an amazing sense to be able to navigate their way home. Remember how, after a few days, the dove flew back with an olive twig in its mouth? Since then, the dove and the olive branch have become symbols of peace.

In the fifth century before Jesus' birth, the Syrians and Persians used pigeons to send important messages. There are ancient engravings of these pigeons in their buildings. Throughout history people have used carrier or homing pigeons to send messages – right up to our great-grandparents' time.

Armies have used animals to help them in their battles. We have seen many paintings of soldiers on horses, but did you know that armies relied on homing pigeons, too? They don't use them today because we have all kinds of ways to send messages via telecommunications.

There is a story of a very famous homing pigeon from the First World War that saved just under two hundred American soldiers in 1918.

Five hundred American soldiers were stranded in the Battle of Argonne. Many had been killed by the enemy – and, even worse, they were being attacked by their friends or allies who thought they were the enemy. It was a desperate situation. The soldiers were without food. They had run out of bullets for their guns. All they had were three homing pigeons. They decided to send one out to their allies for help. It was shot. They sent the second one out: it was shot, too. Only the third one, which they called Cher Ami, which in French means 'dear friend', was left. They loved Cher Ami, but they had no choice but to send her off now. They tied the message to one of her legs. The note gave the coordinates indicating where they were, told the other battalion that their friends were firing at them, and begged them to stop.

Cher Ami lifted off on her way. She was shot at by the enemy as she flew over their line. Despite her wounds, she flew the twenty-five miles in twenty-five minutes to the soldiers who needed to stop firing at them.

The soldiers couldn't believe her bravery when they saw the blood on her feathers, the bullet in her chest, her blinded eye and only one leg. With all those injuries, Cher Ami had saved the rest of the battalion. They were rescued a few days later.

The medics in the battalion nursed Cher Ami and saved her life. Cher Ami was certainly 'a bird of peace'.

Jesus is referred to as 'the Prince of peace', and He calls us to be channels of His peace wherever we are.

PRAYER

Dear Jesus, thank You for showing us what it means to live in peace with each other. Help me always to choose the peaceful option when it seems easier to put up a fight. Amen.

The Canada Goose

THEME

It is Christlike to encourage and be loyal to each other.

BIBLE GEM

'Therefore encourage one another and build each other up.' *1 Thessalonians 5:11*

YOU COULD USE

- A toy, decoys or models of the Canada goose
- Photographs of Canada geese flying in a V formation

ILLUSTRATION

There is a small lake near to where I live, and we often enjoy walking around it. There are several different waterfowl there, but by far the majority are Canada geese. Canada geese, as the name suggests, come from Canada, and they can be found all over North America. These geese are migratory birds. That means that they fly to the warmer states in the south for the winter, and then migrate back again in the spring.

For some reason, lots of Canada geese have flown to the United Kingdom and have made it their home. We don't mind. . . . The more the merrier!

Canada geese are large birds and are easily recognised for the loud honking noises they make. I have read that they also communicate with each other using between ten and twenty different sounds, depending on what they want to tell the rest of the birds in the flock. They are also recognised for flying together in a V formation. This is such a clever way to conserve as much energy as possible in their long flight. The bird in the front must be particularly strong and will do most of the work for the rest of the flock. In the lead, it splits the air current and reduces air pressure on the birds flying behind it. Also, as the goose in the front flaps it wings, it creates an uplift for the goose immediately behind it. This means that every goose is doing its best to make it easier for the bird behind it. While the goose leading the flock must work very hard, the geese behind will honk out loudly to those in front to encourage them. After some time, the goose behind the leader will take its place and give it time to recover.

Something else that is quite remarkable about these birds is the affection they show to each other. For example, if one of the birds becomes ill and can't keep up, a few birds will drop out of the formation with it. They will protect it and stay with it until it is better or until it dies. When they are able, they join another flock on their flight.

The male goose finds a female partner when he is about three years old, and he stays loyal to her until either he or she dies. He will not leave her in order to mate with other females.

These birds have a keen sense of family too. When the young goslings are about two to three months old, they fly with their parents to the place where they hatched. The family stays united and connected much longer than those of other birds.

There are so many wonderful examples here where the geese do their best to make life easier for the rest of the flock, and also stay loyal to their mates and families. I like that. If a bird can follow the counsel in the Bible to encourage and build each other up, then why can't we?

Let's be encouragers, champion builders of people!

PRAYER

Dear Jesus, thank You for these amazing birds that remind us to be encouragers by building up those around us. Help me to begin, today, to do the same. Amen.

The Sparrow

THEME

God loves me.

BIBLE GEM

'Are not two sparrows sold for a penny? Yet not one of them will fall to the ground outside your Father's care.' *Matthew 10:29*

YOU COULD USE

- Photographs of sparrows
- Download the sparrow bird call from the internet for the children to listen to.

ILLUSTRATION

[Play the bird call.] Isn't that a lovely sound? Do you know what it is? [Let the children respond.] Do you know which bird sings that song? [Don't give it away just yet.]

[Tell them you will read the clue to them from Matthew 10:29.] From the verse we just read in the Bible, you can tell that sparrows were very common birds; there were lots of them, and they were cheap to buy. Sparrows are not very colourful, though the males have interesting markings. [Show the photographs of the sparrows.] They are small birds, but they are also very social birds. They live together in large flocks. They were first found in North Africa, but are now found in Europe, Asia, North America, Australia and New Zealand. Sparrows like living close to humans and can be found in town gardens and parks. They like pecking at the crumbs and morsels people throw out for them. They are not afraid of people, and will happily peck away at the crumbs people have left on garden tables while they are still sitting at them. It is interesting to watch them and pick out their temperaments.

Unlike swallows, sparrows do not migrate. They tend to stay close to their nesting area, apart from the late summer, when they feed on the grain in the fields in the countryside.

I always thought that the sparrow must be one of the most common birds in the world. You could count on them being in every garden. However, something terrible happened in the 1990s. Year after year there were fewer sparrows in Britain, until there were hardly any at all. In some areas of Britain their numbers have fallen by 99%. That is most of them! I miss seeing them.

Ornithologists (people who study birds) don't know the real reason for their disappearance. Some think it may be the pollution from cars; others think it may be the mobile phone masts. Some say the pesticides the farmers used to spray their crops wiped them out, because sparrows eat lots of insects. Others say the rise in the number of cats people keep as pets is responsible. Cats are the sparrows' number-one predators. We still do not know the reason for their huge decline.

It has always been such a joy to see the humble little sparrows again when I have visited other countries.

The Bible verse we read earlier says that, even though sparrows are common and not especially pretty, God cares for them and notes when each is one is ill. Sometimes we think we are nothing special, just an ordinary person like a common sparrow – but God knows everything about us, and He cares about us.

When I was little, we used to sing this song:
'God sees the little sparrow fall;
It meets His tender view:
For God so loved the little birds,
I know He loves me too.
Chorus:
He loves me too, He loves me too, I know He loves me too.
God sees the little sparrow fall; I know He loves me too.
God made the little birds and flowers
And all things large and small;
He'll not forget His little ones:
I know He loves them all.'

Never forget this: *God loves you!*

PRAYER

Thank You for loving me. Amen.

The Swan

THEME

God is faithful to us and He protects us.

BIBLE GEM

'Let love and faithfulness never leave you; bind them round your neck, write them on the tablet of your heart.' *Proverbs 3:3*

YOU COULD USE

- A toy swan
- A swan ornament
- An enlarged photograph of a swan

ILLUSTRATION

Swans are often associated with purity because of their white feathers. They are also associated with loyalty because they mate for life and guard each other, their nests and their babies (called cygnets) closely. They don't cheat on each other.

Swans are the largest of the birds related to ducks and geese. They are also some of the heaviest flying birds. Some can weigh up to 15 kilograms. When their necks are outstretched, they can be as long as one and a half metres. When their wings are fully outstretched, they can reach about 3 metres. That is more than the height of a tall human!

Swans can fly up to 60 miles per hour. That is double the speed cars are allowed to travel on roads in built-up areas.

Swans have very good memories. They remember those who have treated them well and those who haven't. They will attack anyone they think will hurt them.

On 31 July every year a traditional royal practice of counting the Queen's swans on the River Thames takes place. It is known as 'Swan Upping'. The Queen's Swan Uppers (rowers) travel in traditional wooden rowing boats. They are dressed in blue or red blazers bearing the royal insignia. Some sailors push white swan feathers into their caps.

In 1482 only very wealthy people could keep swans on their estates. These birds had to have their beaks marked to show who owned them. Unmarked swans were automatically owned by the king or queen, as they still are today. It is against the law to bother them or kill them. Anyone caught troubling them or killing them is issued with a hefty fine.

Even though there are records of more than 2,000 mute swans on the River Thames in 1496, there were only around 1,300 about 50 years ago, and they dropped even further to just seven pairs by 1985. Why, despite the law of the Queen's protection covering them, were so few left?

This was due to the pollution in the river, the lead fishing weights that poisoned them and fishing lines and hooks. The river was cleaned, and education programmes to save the swans were set up for use in schools and various fishing clubs. Year on year, the numbers of swans on the river have increased since then, but it will still take a long time to see two-thousand-odd swans gliding down the river again.

Isn't it amazing that, for more than six hundred years, the kings and queens have been committed to protecting these remarkably faithful birds? Do you know, Jesus offers us His kingly protection, too? He sees His purity in us, and He tells us that He will love us forever. Are you willing to tell Him that you will love Him forever? Why not tell Him, now, that you will be faithful to Him?

PRAYER

Jesus, thank You for faithfully protecting me. I promise to be faithful to You. Amen.

The Hummingbird

THEME

God expects us to be diligent.

BIBLE GEM

'Whatever you do, work at it with all your heart, as working for the Lord.' *Colossians 3:23*

YOU COULD USE

- Photographs of different hummingbirds

ILLUSTRATION

There aren't hummingbirds where I live, but I was fascinated by these amazing little birds when I visited the United States. Their beautiful, shimmering feathers are stunning, and the movements of their wings are quite hypnotising!

The hummingbird is unusual in so many ways. It gets its name from the whirring or humming sound the wings make, not from its singing! It is the smallest bird in the world, yet it burns up so much energy in flying that it must eat every ten minutes and consume twice its body weight every day. Imagine eating twice your weight every day!

It draws up the sugar from the nectar in the flowers through its long, tube-shaped beak and gets protein from small insects. It catches these by extending its long, thin tongue. On the tip of its tongue are small spines that are used to stab the insects it feeds on.

Hummingbirds can beat their wings up to two hundred times per second. They can fly forwards and backwards and sideways, up and down, and they can even hover like a helicopter! They can fly up to thirty-four miles per hour and can dive at sixty miles per hour.

What strikes one most about these birds is their efficiency and industry. They remember all the flowers and feeders they have visited, and make a point of visiting these in their search for food. This saves a lot of time.

There are several texts in the Bible that encourage us to work hard and not to be lazy, and especially so when we work for Jesus.

PRAYER

Dear Jesus, thank You for all the little pointers from nature that remind me to put all my effort into everything I do to be a blessing to others. Amen.

The Great Barrier Reef

THEME

God is our great Protector.

BIBLE GEM

'But the Lord is faithful, and he will strengthen you and protect you from the evil one.' *2 Thessalonians 3:3*

YOU COULD USE

- Photographs of the Great Barrier Reef
- Natural sponges and examples of coral (only if you have them)
- Photographs of some of the animals from the Great Barrier Reef

ILLUSTRATION

The Great Barrier Reef is one of the most amazing wonders of nature – it will make you gasp! It is the largest coral ecosystem in the world, entirely made by living organisms. It lies in the shallow (about sixty metres deep), warm waters off the coastline of Queensland, Northern Australia. It stretches across 2,600 kilometres, and lies about fifteen kilometres from the mainland at its closest point and 150 kilometres at its furthest point. Nature has created the ideal conditions for the 400 different kinds of coral that grow there, creating a home for over 1,500 different kinds of fish; 4,000 kinds of molluscs (sea creatures with shells); mammals like the dugong; sharks and dolphins; reptiles like crocodiles, sea-snakes and turtles; other animals like sponges; sea plants; and 215 different types of birds and forests.

Try to imagine how big the Great Barrier Reef is – think how big a football pitch is, and multiply that by 70 million! Doesn't that make you want to say, 'Wow!' Try and imagine it another way – it is a similar size to the whole state of California or the entire country of Finland.

The reef is made up of over a thousand different islands created by the coral, and 2,500 individual reefs.

In 1981 it was declared a World Heritage Area. That means that it is such a precious gift of nature that we need to protect it from being lost forever.

In 2011 it was shortlisted in a competition for a place in one of the seven natural wonders of the world. It wasn't included in the final seven, though it is hard to understand why it missed it.

The Barrier Reef is home to some of the animals and plants we are learning about in this book, like the hermit crab, the sea anemone and the clownfish.

Sadly, the Great Barrier Reef is in danger of being destroyed and lost. Buildings that are damaged or destroyed can be repaired and rebuilt, but the coral reefs are made by tiny organisms, and when they are destroyed the coral dies. We cannot put them back together again. We all need to play our part in taking care of the beautiful world God gave us.

Since 1985 the Barrier Reef has lost half its coral. The fertilisers and pesticides sprayed on the farm crops in Northern Australia drain into the rivers and flow out to sea. When they flow into the reef, they kill the tiny organisms that keep the coral alive and give it its vibrant colour. Equally, climate change, pollution from large ships, overfishing and disturbances in the water from excavating in the sea when building large seaports have all contributed to the fragile state of the Barrier Reef.

I think of the Great Barrier Reef as an underwater paradise, a place of safety for so many different life forms. Like a huge, friendly giant it seems to wrap its great protective arms around everything within it, saying, 'Stay with me. You will always be safe in my arms.'

In a way, God offers us protection from the harm the evil one puts in our path, and He says to us, 'Stay with Me. You will always be safe in My arms.'

PRAYER

Protect me from the evil one. . . . Keep me safe in Jesus' name. Amen.

The Hermit Crab

THEME

We need each other to live happy, healthy lives.

BIBLE GEM

'In response to all he has done for us, let us outdo each other in being helpful and kind to each other and in doing good.' *Hebrews 10:24 (TLB)*

YOU COULD USE

- Downloaded and enlarged photographs of the hermit crab and sea anemones

ILLUSTRATION

When I visit the ocean, I often like to scurry among the rocks to look at the different creatures in the rock pools. Some of my favourites are the hermit crabs. They are unusual crabs because they do not have their own shells like other crabs do. Females lay their eggs on the ocean floor. As soon as an egg hatches, the young hermit crab must fend for itself and make its own way. The first thing it will do is find an empty snail shell that it will move into. It uses a substance from its mouth to coat the inside of the shell, which will help it to stay attached. As it grows, it will find a larger shell to move into until it is fully grown.

When they pull themselves into their shells, they have to twist themselves into a spiral shape and then fold themselves safely inside.

Hermit crabs are found in the ocean, and on land. They breathe through gills, and those on land must find water for their gills to keep them working well. They have ten long legs and two large claws, which they use for catching their food. A pair of eyes sit on top of two long stalks, and they have two antennae to help them feel their way around the rocks.

Hermit crabs are nocturnal – that means that they stay undercover in the day and go exploring at night. They are not fussy eaters, and will eat plankton, tiny sea creatures, fruits and vegetables.

Hermit crabs are not hermits. They do not like living alone. In fact, hermit crabs that live on their own do not usually live for more than a year. By contrast, hermit crabs that live with other hermit crabs can live for up to forty years! It just goes to show that we need each other to live happy, healthy lives!

Another fascinating fact about the hermit crab is that it will often attach a young sea anemone to its shell, even from the first tiny shell, and they often live together for life. When the hermit crab moves to another shell it takes its sea anemone partner with it. They benefit each other hugely. The sea anemone picks up more food with its tentacles as the hermit crab moves about the rocks. On the other hand, the sea anemone protects the hermit crab by shooting out its stingers when predators are close by.

Hermit crabs also like variety and a change of scenery. Don't we all? That is what makes life so interesting!

The hermit crab reminds us that we do not live in a vacuum; we cannot live well without sharing company with others. Loneliness can make us ill. In our text, we are reminded to be kind and helpful to each other and to do good. What a good idea!

PRAYER

Help me to be a friend like You, Jesus. Amen.

The Clownfish

THEME

We are all important to God, especially the young.

BIBLE GEM

' "Let the little children come to me, and do not hinder them. . . ." And he took the children in his arms . . . and blessed them.' *Mark 10:14, 16*

YOU COULD USE

- Plastic or furry Nemo toys
- Photographs of clownfish
- Photographs of a sea anemone

ILLUSTRATION

How many of you have seen the film about Nemo? Have any of you read a book about Nemo? Who was Nemo? Did he look like one of these? [Show the children the toy or photograph.] Nemo was a clownfish.

Do you know where clownfish live? They are mostly found in warm oceans and seas like the Pacific Ocean, the Indian Ocean and the Red Sea, and there are loads of them in the Great Barrier Reef.

Just like the hermit crab, the clownfish and the sea anemone make good partners. They live close together and support each other. The clownfish helps the sea anemone by eating the parasites and dead tentacles on the anemone. This makes space for small creatures to get closer to it so that it can catch and eat them. On the other hand, the sea anemone provides the clownfish with various snacks and, best of all, it protects the clownfish from predators by stinging them with its poisonous tentacles. This is just as well, because clownfish aren't the best swimmers.

Did you know that all clownfish are born male? When they partner, one will turn itself into a female. The father prepares the 'nest' for the mother and guards it. He guards the eggs when they are laid and then keeps the nest clean from anything that might float into it. It makes perfect sense when mammals take such care over their young, but to think that a small daddy fish will be so protective of his young is quite extraordinary.

Jesus is just as protective of His children. When the disciples tried to send them away, Jesus told them to bring them back to Him. He held them and blessed them. Today, He is preparing a home for us in heaven, and He has made sure there is room for everyone. It won't be long before He'll say to you, 'My beautiful child, it's time to go home! Let's go. . . .' I'm looking forward to that! Are you?

PRAYER

Thank You for being my loving Father and for blessing me. Amen.

The Salmon's Incredible Journey

sermon **30**

THEME

To win the race, we need determination and perseverance.

BIBLE GEM

'Let us run with perseverance the race marked out for us, fixing our eyes on Jesus, the pioneer and perfecter of faith.' *Hebrews 12:1, 2*

YOU COULD USE

- A plastic model of a salmon (some fishmongers may let you borrow one)
- Photographs and/or books about salmon

ILLUSTRATION

The salmon, a large fish, lays its eggs in the gravel of riverbeds under fast-flowing water. After a few days, the females that laid the eggs die, but the story does not end there! After two to three years, the small fish that hatched from the eggs swim downstream to the ocean, where they will find plenty to eat. Then, fully grown, when the time comes for those fish to lay their eggs, the salmon will swim all the way back to the place where they were hatched in their freshwater gravel riverbeds.

Their journeys are not straightforward, and they must face dangers of many kinds. They have to swim upstream against the current; this means they have to be strong enough not to be swept back. They must leap up several waterfalls, which they do in stages if the waterfall is very high. They must avoid predators like bears, eagles, and canny fishermen with their fishing lines. This long, tough journey can be several thousand miles.

How do they know to do that? Some say they smell their way; others say it has to do with the sun and electrical charges from the currents in the ocean. Others know that God designed their DNA that way.

As Jesus' followers, we could compare our life journey to that of the salmon. In a world where people are going a certain way that may not be good, we must face them head-on and go against the stream. Some of these people are our friends, and they cannot understand why we won't join them in their journey. Sometimes Satan is successful in luring us, like the canny fisherman does when he catches a salmon: but Jesus can help us to avoid being caught when we allow Him to.

We know that God's plan for our lives is to live with Him forever. He tells us to persevere, not to give in, and to stay on the course He has set for us. Just as the salmon swim night and day until they reach their spawning grounds, we must stay focused on Jesus night and day until we reach the end of our journey.

PRAYER

Dear Jesus, You have a plan for my life – show me where to go, and help me to persevere with determination to the very end of the journey. Amen.

The Squid

sermon

31

THEME

We cannot judge someone's character by their outward appearance.

BIBLE GEM

'But the LORD said to Samuel, "Do not consider his appearance. . . . The LORD does not look at the things people look at. People look at the outward appearance, but the LORD looks at the heart." '
1 Samuel 16:7

YOU COULD USE

- A real squid if you live close to the ocean
- A plastic toy squid
- Enlarged photographs of a squid

ILLUSTRATION

I must be honest: there is nothing about a squid that I find attractive. Yet, apart from their looks, they are interesting because of their unique features that enable them to survive and thrive in the oceans. So many other species are in danger of extinction or are, at least, in decline, but the squid have amazing ways to adapt so that they are not endangered. Did you know that there are over 300 different species of squid? Even though we do not see them very often, there is no shortage of them in the ocean. They range in size, too, from the size of a fingernail to the giants that can grow to more than 40 feet long. Most squid are as long as about two rulers end-to-end. Squid belong to the cephalopod group and are similar to octopi.

They have four pairs of arms, which they use for grabbing things, and two longer tentacles with suckers to help them to move. If they lose an arm, they can grow another one.

They have brains at the front of their heads, though no nervous system or skeleton.

What makes these animals so interesting is that they feed deep down on the ocean beds where there is no light. To help them to see where they are going when they hunt for food, they have glow-in-the-dark organs which light up. This makes their bodies see-through, and they have all the light they need to see.

Besides these 'glow-in-the-dark' organs, they have the biggest eyes of all animals to help them to see where there is very little light. Their eyes have hard, inbuilt contact lenses which work like magnifying glasses. They are very well equipped to feed in the darkest, deepest waters.

They also have a clever way of tricking their predators by shooting out an inky liquid that appears in the same shape and size as the squid. This tricks the predator into thinking they are there when they are not, as they have already made their escape.

Humboldt squid can turn bright red in an instant to hide from their predators. Turning red, at the bottom of the ocean where there is no light, makes them invisible.

It seems that, no matter what difficulty comes their way, they have a trick up their sleeve to get around it.

My initial unease about these creatures changed into admiration when I found out more about their capabilities. Their strange looks didn't matter any more!

When Samuel was asked to seek out a king for the Israelites, God reminded him not to look on his outward appearance. God would help him select the person with the right character and heart.

Isaiah warned that there would be nothing remarkable about the outer appearance of the Messiah, but His character, His love and His wisdom would set Him above anyone else (Isaiah 53).

How often do we think a handsome or beautiful, smartly dressed person is more important than the homeless person with his dog in the subway? Jesus reminds us that He died for all and He loves all. Only He knows our hearts.

Will you be like Jesus and love each person you meet as a child of God?

PRAYER

Dear Jesus, thank You for creating me in Your image. Help me to remember that everyone I meet was created in Your image, too. Help me not to judge anyone by their outward appearance, because only You know what is in their heart. Amen.

Whales

THEME

Jesus' love is so great that He died to rescue us from sin.

BIBLE GEM

'For God so loved the world that he gave his one and only Son, that whoever believes in him shall not perish but have eternal life.' *John 3:16*

YOU COULD USE

- Toy whales
- Enlarged photographs of grey whales, preferably showing their distinctive features

ILLUSTRATION

Have any of you watched a whale? What type of whale was it? Did you know that there are 19 different species of whale? Grey whales are half the size of blue whales. That does not mean that they are small. They're 14 metres long [you could measure that length in the building to give the children a better idea] and they weigh 32,000 kilograms! How much do you weigh? [Try to draw some comparisons.] You can recognise grey whales by the 8-14 ridges along their backs. They have baleen plates, not teeth: arranged in groups of two, there could be any number of pairs between 130 and 150.

Lots of animals and birds migrate. Whales do too. It is said that grey whales travel the furthest of any mammal in their migration, which is about 10,000 miles. Their migration from the feeding grounds begins in October and ends in the Gulf of California or Baja California, where the birthing grounds are.

Grey whales are canny! They can recognise the song of the orca whales, their natural predators. As soon as they hear one, they dart off and hide among the kelp.

Mother grey whales take excellent care of their young, and teach them all the skills they need to take care of themselves and to avoid danger. When their young have shown that they have learned all the skills, the mother gives them their independence and they are free to take care of themselves. It takes her about six to seven months to rear her young.

Some years ago, televisions beamed out news reports of three young grey whales that were stranded and hemmed in by ice off the coast of Alaska. It seemed that the whole world wanted to be on hand to help rescue them!

The whales had been feeding there in the Bering Sea through the summer, and should have begun to make their long migratory journey to Mexico's Baja. Now they were trapped, surrounded by ice. They were in trouble!

It was important that everyone involved in rescuing the grey whales got the timing right. Freeing the trapped whales was only one part of the mission. While the whales were trapped, they needed to create vents in the ice so the whales could breathe. Local Inuit hunters took care of that. When these holes began to freeze over, water pumps were used to keep the water moving so it would not freeze. Amazingly, the whales followed the noise of the pumps, which led them to the vents where they could breathe.

On the Russian side of the ice, icebreakers used chainsaws to make a channel several miles in length as a pathway for the whales to get out to the open sea. It was hazardous, because they had to take great care not to hurt the whales. Only two of the whales eventually made it. As the rescuers coaxed them out to sea, the whales seemed to understand that these humans were helping them.

This heart-warming story reminds us of another rescue mission from 2,000 years ago. God sent His Son, Jesus, to a very troubled world, and asked Him to save everyone in it. He arrived as a baby; shared the good news that we could all live with God in heaven, free from all the bad things that go on around us and that we ourselves do; and then gave His life for us. Isn't that the most amazing rescue mission ever?

PRAYER

Loving Saviour, You didn't just use chainsaws and pumps to rescue me. You gave Your life for me. Thank You. Amen.

Dolphins

THEME

Jesus went out of His way to understand people and to help them.

BIBLE GEM

'Share each other's burdens, and in this way obey the law of Christ. If you think you are too important to help someone, you are only fooling yourself.' *Galatians 6:2, 3 (NLT)*

YOU COULD USE

- A dolphin soft toy
- A dolphin puppet
- A picture of dolphins

ILLUSTRATION

Did you know that dolphins are often considered to be the second- or third-most intelligent animal after humans? They are sometimes called the dogs of the sea because they are so sociable and playful. Marine scientists and biologists have studied them for many years. Apparently, there are forty-five different species of dolphins, and five of those are river dolphins. They live in groups called pods, with some being as large as one thousand members. They communicate with each other using different squeaks, clicks and whistles.

Dolphins are usually gentle. There are several stories about dolphins saving shipwrecked people or those who have drifted out to sea and find themselves in danger.

I met a student at college who had run into difficulty with a group of friends when their boat capsized off the coast of Mozambique. She was a powerful swimmer, but she quickly grew tired trying to swim back to the shore. A dolphin spotted her and pushed her onto a buoy, where she stayed until the rescue boat found her!

I heard about a teenager, Davide, who fell from the side of his parents' boat on the South-East Italian coast. Davide was a weak swimmer. He was about to drown when a dolphin spotted him and swam under him. When Davide realised that the dolphin was pushing him up and out of the water, he held on to it as it swam to the boat, where his dad was able to pull him up to safety. What a powerful example of empathy!

Jesus was the Master Empathiser! In an instant He knew how someone felt, and He understood what they were going through. Remember the story of the woman who had done bad things, whom the men were about to stone? Jesus wrote some of the bad things those men had done in the sand, and they slunk off in shame. Jesus told her that she had been forgiven and that she was never to do those bad things again. It is likely that she felt understood and loved, and that Jesus' act of empathy changed her heart.

Wouldn't it be wonderful if all humans behaved the same way towards each other?

PRAYER

Help me to notice what others are going through and to encourage them. Amen.

The Giant Sequoias

sermon 34

We can withstand life's challenges and be people of sound character when we are rooted in Jesus.

BIBLE GEM

'So then, just as you received Christ Jesus as Lord, continue to live your lives in him, rooted and built up in him, strengthened in the faith as you were taught, and overflowing with thankfulness.' *Colossians 2:6, 7*

YOU COULD USE

- Photographs of sequoias
- Lengths of rope to show the diameter and measurement across the larger sequoias
- Open and closed cones

ILLUSTRATION

It is impossible to imagine a world without any trees. How dull it would be! Even worse, it would spell the end of life on our planet, because trees, as well as other plants, filter the air and keep it clean for us to breathe and survive.

Some of the most amazing trees on our planet are the giant sequoias. They are the largest trees in the world. They are unusual in so many ways, because they can live for up to 3,000 years and outlast any other tree. This is because the high percentage of tannin in their bark allows them to resist disease and fungal rot, to resist the insects that like to tunnel their way into bark, and to resist fire. Their bark can grow up to three feet thick. Did you know that they can be as tall as a 26-storey building? They can grow to more than 20 feet in diameter.

The largest sequoia is called 'General Sherman', which is said to weigh 2.7 million pounds.

The sequoia can only grow from a seed. The soil conditions must be just right for the approximate 91,000 seeds that will drop from a cone to germinate. The soil must be bare mineral soil, and the soil is only ever this way after a fire. A fire will also burn off competition, giving the seeds a good head start. The fire helps the cone to burst open so that the seeds are released.

Giant sequoias are designed to cope with fires. The thick outer bark protects the rest of the tree from being burned and insulates it from the heat. When fire manages to reach the new growth and cause some scarring, the new rapid growth on the tree covers the scar completely so that it is completely protected again.

These amazing trees remind us that our characters can flourish in the same way. Sometimes the struggles in our life seem to rage like a destructive fire, but the inner strength God gives us, like tannin in the bark of the sequoia, fireproofs us, and the new growth covers the scars completely. It reminds us that God sometimes uses those struggles to clear away the things that stunt us and compete for the space that will hinder our growth. These amazing trees remind us that seeds rooted in Jesus will grow strong and tall. Would you like to stand tall for Jesus like General Sherman? Will you make sure that you are rooted in Him?

PRAYER

Dear Father God, root me in Your love and create a firewall around me to be strong in the bad times. Amen.

A Fig Tree and Some Figs

THEME

The fruit of the Spirit is worth having.

BIBLE GEM

'But when the Holy Spirit controls our lives he will produce this kind of fruit in us: love, joy, peace, patience, kindness, goodness, faithfulness, gentleness and self-control.' *Galatians 5:22, 23 (TLB)*

YOU COULD USE

- A basket with a few fresh figs in it
- Some dried figs

ILLUSTRATION

I have some very special fruit in my basket today. [Show the fresh figs.] Did you know that when you eat a fig you are eating an inside-out flower? You can't see the flowers from the outside, but they are all tucked safely inside an outer fleshy layer. If you want to be really smart you would say that this type of flower is *infructescent*!

Another interesting fact about figs is that they are pollinated by a special type of wasp. The wasp enters the flower through a tiny passage [show it on another fig] and it is eventually dissolved, so you do not eat it when the fruit is ripe.

Figs are rich in fibre, minerals and vitamins, and they can be eaten fresh, like these, or as dried fruit. They can be served as a sweet or eaten as part of a savoury meal.

Figs are used for other purposes too. They make good cough medicine. They make good face masks because they tighten the skin. Juice taken from the leaves is good for soothing insect bites. Figs are

74

helpful to those who want to give up smoking because they are alkaline, and this reduces the craving for the nicotine in cigarettes.

Did you know that the edible fig tree was the first plant humans cultivated? Its roots grow near the surface of the ground, though its diameter is three times wider than the crown! The several varieties of fig trees grown in South Africa have roots that grow deep into the soil.

Jesus taught a lesson from the fig tree. It was a barren tree. A man had planted a fig tree in his garden. He went out to pick some figs, but, when he got to the tree, he couldn't find one! He was fed up and told his gardener that the tree had not borne any fruit for three years, and he asked him to dig it up and get rid of it. The gardener advised him to be patient and asked him to give it another chance for a year. He promised to nurture it by digging the soil around it and fertilising it. If, after all that help, it still did not bear fruit, he would cut the tree down.

Through this parable Jesus showed how that fig tree is like many of us. We get on with our lives, but we aren't really going anywhere. Our spiritual lives are empty, and we are not producing fruit. We are not helping others to know and love Jesus.

And the gardener is like Jesus. He says, 'I'll give you another chance. I'll do everything I can to help you to bear fruit.' The Bible tells us about the kind of fruit God wants to see in our lives: not figs, but the fruit of the Spirit, which is love, joy, peace, patience, kindness, goodness, faithfulness, gentleness and self-control. This is what God helps us to produce when we turn from our selfish ways and offer to serve Him.

Why not allow Jesus to tend the soil around your tree today so that you will produce the tastiest fruit ever?

PRAYER

Help me to grow so that I will bear good fruit that will be a blessing to others. Amen.

The Horse Chestnut Tree

sermon **36**

THEME

A good character is priceless.

BIBLE GEM

'Do not store up for yourselves treasures on earth, where moths and vermin destroy.'
Matthew 6:19

YOU COULD USE

- Photographs of the horse chestnut tree
- Depending on the season, a few leaf samples and a cluster of flowers, or a few horse chestnuts, some with and some without their shells
- Two conkers prepared for a conker contest (the game children play)

ILLUSTRATION

You won't believe how happy it makes me when the large horse chestnut trees on the avenue near my house suddenly shoot bright, lime-green leaves in the spring. After the long, grey winter, it is a sign that summer is on its way, and I want to sing! The leaves are large and shaped like hands, with five to seven long fingers, and they turn a darker green as days get warmer.

The flowers appear in late spring, when upright candelabra-like panicles of small, white flowers festoon the tree. By autumn these will have produced spikey, round, green fruits that each hold a glossy brown horse chestnut inside. The fruit is not edible, but every autumn children will gather the horse chestnuts to make conkers for their conker contests by punching a hole through each conker and then threading a short piece of string through it. Children form pairs and battle it out to see who has the strongest conker. There is a technique to smashing the opponent's conker by flicking your own at it. The aim is to keep your own conker intact on its string.

There are over two million horse chestnut trees in the United Kingdom. They are not native to our island, but one would be forgiven for thinking that they were. They are large trees, native to the Balkan states in South-East Europe. They were first introduced to line avenues and streets in our major cities. You will find them in parks and gardens all around the country. The reasons for importing them in the first place were that they were so large and majestic; they provided a good canopy of shade; and, best of all, there weren't any insects or diseases that attacked them. That was true then – but, sadly, not any more!

Half our horse chestnut trees suffer either from leaf miner moths that lay their eggs on the leaves, or bleeding canker and leaf blot fungus.

When the caterpillars hatch from the larvae of the leaf miner moth, they burrow into the leaf and destroy the chlorophyll. Chlorophyll is the green substance in the leaf that traps the energy from the sun and helps plants grow healthy and strong. The leaves slowly turn a rusty brown colour and die long before they should. They don't have any chance to change to their usual lemon-yellow colour in the autumn. All the trees near where I live have suffered. They seem to suffer more each year.

Bleeding canker, a fungal disease, on the other hand, attacks the bark of the tree. The first sign that something might be wrong is when a sticky sap leaks from the bark on the branches and the trunk. As it gets worse, the bark splits. With each passing year the tree produces fewer leaves, and eventually it dies. There is no treatment that can stop this disease.

It saddens me to think that we could lose these beautiful old trees that have brought so many people so much pleasure for the last two or three centuries. How can it be that something as small as a moth or caterpillar, or a fungal spore you can't even see with the naked eye, could eventually destroy these huge, majestic trees?

Jesus warned us not to put our treasure where moths or vermin could destroy it. By that He meant that we could put all our energy into getting things, thinking that they will make us happy, only to find that even the tiniest of things can destroy everything we have worked for.

At another level, habits we cling to that do us no good act like those pesky leaf miner moths and fungal spores. If we don't give up those bad habits, our characters are spoilt and tarnished before we know it.

Your good character is all you have when everything is stripped away. Guard it; be strong!

PRAYER

Help me to develop only habits of good character. Amen.

The Passionflower

THEME

God loves us.

BIBLE GEM

'For God so loved the world that he gave his one and only Son, that whoever believes in him shall not perish but have eternal life.' *John 3:16*

YOU COULD USE

- A strand from a passion fruit plant with flowers on it, or a small passion fruit plant in flower
- An artificial example of a passionflower
- Coloured photographs of the passionflower
- A passion fruit

ILLUSTRATION

Long ago, more than 400 years ago, some Spanish and Portuguese missionaries who went to the Americas were fascinated by an unusual and beautiful flower that grew on vines there. They couldn't think of any flower back in Europe that even nearly looked like it. They studied it carefully, made drawings of everything they saw, and then noticed that they could use its characteristics to explain the story of Jesus to the native Americans who had not yet learned about Him. [Show the parts of the flower to the children as you explain it.] That is why they called it the passionflower, a flower that reminded them of everything Jesus did for us because He loved us so much.

In the centre of the flower was a single column that reminded them how Jesus had been whipped. The tendrils around the plant reminded them of the whips that were used to beat Him.

The three stigma with rounded heads reminded them of the nails used to fasten Jesus' hands and feet to the cross.

The five anthers reminded them of five places where He was wounded at the crucifixion – these were the wounds in both His hands, His feet and His side where a soldier had pierced Him with his spear.

The rays that formed a halo reminded them that He was God.

The ten petals reminded them of the apostles who were faithful to Jesus. Judas had betrayed Him for thirty pieces of silver, and Peter had fled in fear after lying and saying that he had never known Jesus.

Finally, the round fruit, the passion fruit, reminded them of the world Jesus had come to save.

The missionaries brought the plant back to Spain, and now you will find it growing in many gardens all over Europe and the world – even in my garden!

The missionaries used the passionflower to help their listeners understand the story. However it is explained, it is a powerful story of forgiveness, grace and love that changes the hearts of men and women, boys and girls to this very day! Have you opened your heart to Him?

PRAYER

Dear Jesus, You died a cruel death to give me life, and now I open my heart to You. Amen.

Sunflowers

THEME

We are happy when we follow Jesus.

BIBLE GEM

'This is the day the Lord has made. We will rejoice and be glad in it.' *Psalm 118:24 (TLB)*

YOU COULD USE

- A real sunflower or a few of them
- Artificial sunflowers (you can find inexpensive examples at craft and hobby stores)
- Some sunflower seeds – black, striped or both – and just the kernels

ILLUSTRATION

I love seeing all the sunflowers in the gardens, allotments and stores at this time of year! They are such cheerful plants that brighten up our world. Six months ago, this sunflower was just a seed like this. It was planted in the ground. It grew quickly, because sunflowers are one of the fastest-growing plants. In that time, it grew taller than your parents or anyone you know. In fact, it grew at least two feet taller than most of your dads. Sunflowers can grow up to twelve feet tall in those six months.

From that one small seed it will have made one to two thousand little flowers in the centre. The yellow part of the flower is not made of petals, but of sepals. Each one of those tiny flowers in the centre forms a seed. From one small seed it grew one to two thousand seeds. Isn't that a good return for very little effort? Depending on the variety, those seeds may be black or striped. [Show the children the seeds.]

The seeds are very nutritious and are used in several different ways. For example, the oil is extracted from the black seed, and this is used for cooking oil, as a supplement for animal food, in hair products to make it healthy and glossy, and in creams used for healing wounds.

The striped seeds are left in their shells for bird food and shelled for eating. Sometimes we see them in our bread, our muesli, in cookies and in energy bars, because they are good for us. Roasted sunflower seeds are delicious, too. The seeds are packed with calcium and iron and vitamins A and D, which are important for our health.

The botanical name for the sunflower is *Helianthus*. *Helia* is the Greek word for the sun, and *anthus* is the Greek word for 'flower'. People gave them that name because sunflowers turn their heads to face the sun. Early in the morning they will face east, where the sun rises, and by sunset they will face it going down in the west. It is easy to see why the flower has become a symbol of faith, loyalty and adoration.

As children of God, when we turn our faces to Him and follow Him, we can do amazing things: we bring peace and cheer to those around us; we help those who are ill or sad. We bring health and healing.

You may be just one small sunflower seed right now, but just think about how quickly you can turn that seed into a tall, healthy plant bearing such a huge flower of goodness.

As the sunflower begins its day turned to the sun, we can begin ours turned to the Son. We can be happy and thank Jesus for the day He has given us, and promise to use it to make others happy, too.

PRAYER

Just as the sunflower turns its face to the sun, help me to turn to You and to follow You today, Jesus. Amen.

Lemons

Our influence can be far more positive than we can ever imagine.

BIBLE GEM

'By their fruit you will recognise them.' *Matthew 7:16*

YOU COULD USE

- A bowl of fresh lemons
- A small fruit salad
- A squeeze of lemon in the fruit salad as you develop the illustration

ILLUSTRATION

What is your favourite fruit? [Let the children tell you.] Why is it your favourite? Is it the flavour? Is because it is juicy? Does it feel nice on your tongue? I like all fruit, but there is one fruit that is my favourite. Would you like to have a taste of it? [You could get a child to dip their finger in some lemon juice, or just leave it.] [Show them the bowl of lemons.] Aren't they beautiful? Pick one from the bowl and smell it. I just love the smell of lemon. It smells fresh and clean and even makes me feel like smiling.

Now, I wouldn't peel this lemon and eat it like an orange or a clementine. I couldn't do that. So why are lemons such a favourite of mine? You see, a little squeeze of fresh lemon in this fruit salad will make all the other fruits you like taste even better! It makes a difference to all the other fruits. I like squeezing lemons on my green vegetables. It makes them taste even nicer. I like adding a lemon dressing to my salads, which makes them more flavourful. I like shredding some of the lemon peel and adding it to the cake batter or biscuit dough when I bake. It gives my cakes and biscuits a zing, and they smell wonderful!

Lemons are quite extraordinary. I think that they are nature's little insect repellents, because insects won't come near you if you rub some of the oil from the peel onto your skin: not only that, but they have antibacterial properties and help to fight the bacteria when you have a sore throat. For the same reason, they are good for indigestion. People who make cleaning products often add lemon juice to the mixture because it gets rid of any lingering bad smells.

What is more, lemons contain lots of potassium, which is good for keeping our hearts healthy.

When Jesus explained what the fruit of the Spirit was to His friends, He told them that they would be known by their fruits. If they were kind, their fruit would be kindness; if they were patient, their fruit would be patience; if there they were angry, their fruit would be anger; and if they were selfish, their fruit would be selfishness.

Just as a banana would taste like a banana, and not an apple, the reason why I like lemons is that they not only taste like lemons, but they can make a banana or an apple taste even better. Jesus asks us not only to produce 'good fruit', but to help other 'good fruit' taste even better! Do you think you could?

PRAYER

Dear Jesus, help me to produce good 'fruit' and to help those around me to be more pleasant too. Amen.

Vineyards and Grapevines

sermon 40

BIBLE GEM

'Yes, I am the Vine; you are the branches. Whoever lives in me and I in him shall produce a large crop of fruit.' *John 15:5 (TLB)*

YOU COULD USE

- A vine branch (preferably real, but artificial will do)
- Some different varieties of grapes (colours, shapes and sizes)
- A dead branch from a fruit tree

ILLUSTRATION

Can you guess which is one of the largest food industries in the world? [Allow the children to respond, and then show them the samples of grapes you have brought with you.]

There are more than sixty species of grape worldwide. Can you guess how many varieties there are? There are 8,000! Each one has a slightly different shape, colour, size and taste!

Grapes are grown for eating. I love popping a crisp, juicy grape between my teeth. They are also preserved in jars or cans and turned into jams and syrups. They are dried into raisins, and mostly they are crushed for juice. Grapes are 80% water, but raisins are dried, so they are only 15% water.

Grapes are amazingly good for us and for keeping us healthy. They are good for our brains, our lungs, our hearts, our kidneys and our stomachs.

Grapevines typically have a main stem or trunk, and the branches that grow from these are tied to horizontal wires; the bunches of grapes grow out of the branches. They start out as tiny green spheres, smaller than a garden pea, and gradually swell and finally change colour as they are ripened in the hot sun.

Jesus lived in Palestine, where the weather is just right for growing grape vines. There were loads of vineyards, and most people knew a lot about how to grow and care for them. He told them a story about grapevines. Pointing to the vineyard, he reminded them that the branches must be connected to the vine or the trunk. If a branch is broken or cut off from the vine, it will be impossible for the branch to produce bunches of grapes. [Show the dead branch.] This branch is dead. It was damaged in a storm and was torn away from the tree. It can never produce fruit. Just like this branch, anyone who is torn or cut away from Jesus cannot produce fruit. Jesus said that He is the Vine, and only as we are connected to Him do we produce fruit.

We won't produce bunches of grapes, but He expects our fruit to be in the form of love, joy, peace, patience, kindness, goodness, faithfulness, gentleness and self-control. Only Jesus will produce this fruit of the Holy Spirit in us.

Stay connected to Jesus so that your branches will be laden with fruit!

PRAYER

Dear Jesus, thank You for being a strong, sturdy vine. Keep me connected to You and bearing the best fruit ever! Amen.

The Calla Lily (41)

THEME

Do not place value on others based on where they come from, but rather on who they are.

BIBLE GEM

'Do not judge others, so that God will not judge you, for God will judge you in the same way as you judge others, and he will apply to you the same rules you apply to others.' *Matthew 7:1, 2 (GNB)*

YOU COULD USE

- Either a fresh calla lily (available at garden centres and even service stations) or an artificial one

ILLUSTRATION

Whenever I see a calla lily, I am reminded of how much we took them for granted when I was a child, because they grew in abundance in the wild near where we lived. They were large, sturdy plants with thick, glossy leaves, crowned with the most amazing creamy-white, funnel-shaped flowers. Almost modernist, I loved their designer-minimalist quality. They are often used for wedding bouquets. They are often used in arrangements at church for the Easter services, because they have become a symbol of Jesus' resurrection. They also symbolise innocence and purity: qualities Jesus possessed and which we admire. The calla lily often represents purity and holiness in medieval Christian paintings. See if you can spot one when you next visit an art gallery.

Calla lilies come in a variety of colours now, but they were originally only available in white, symbolising purity of thought.

What we call the flower is not a flower at all! It is a modified leaf called a spathe. There are loads of very tiny flowers inside the spathe that grow on the narrow flower spike.

Flower arrangers love these plants, but they are considered very common in their homeland in South Africa, where they grow in marshy, unattractive places. It is a marvel that something so simple and beautiful can rise out of all the litter and mud.

It reminds me of the account in the Bible where Nathanael asks Philip, 'Can any good come out of Nazareth?' with reference to Jesus growing up there. Nathanael obviously thought that a certain type of person came from Nazareth, and he didn't seem impressed. He had formed a judgement before he had even met Jesus. Often, we fall into the same trap. We make judgements based on where people come from, the part of town where they live, or the type of clothes they wear. Jesus reminds us that we are not to judge others, but to accept them for who they are. Pure, and clean, Jesus lived God's way.

Will you choose to live a pure, clean life as Jesus did? Will you be accepting of everyone and leave the judging to God?

PRAYER

Just as the calla lily rises clean and pure from the mud and dirt, help me to remember that purity comes from within. Amen.

Roses and Rose Oil

THEME

Like Jesus, we can be an influence for good and a blessing to others.

BIBLE GEM

'Follow God's example, therefore, as dearly loved children and live a life of love, just as Christ loved us and gave himself up for us as a fragrant offering and sacrifice to God.' *Ephesians 5:1, 2*

YOU COULD USE

- Roses of different colours and shapes
- Some rose water poured onto a piece of cotton wool
- A bottle of perfume with rose oil as one of the ingredients (most good floral brands do have rose oil)

ILLUSTRATION

I love roses. Do you? I like them because they come in so many different colours and shades, shapes and sizes. In my garden I have some roses that produce large buds that are good for cutting and arranging in a vase. I have some that carry soft, fragile blooms that are best left on the plant. These are the size of small trees now! The shrub or tree is covered in flowers all through the summer and into the autumn, and their perfume is amazing. I love opening the doors and letting their fragrance waft into the house. One rose bush in my garden, a climber that doesn't have any thorns, has the tiniest, daintiest roses I have ever seen. It flowers in the late spring – not for very long, but the foliage is still pretty all through the summer.

Did you know that there are over one hundred species of rose around the world? Of those, there are hundreds of different hybrids. The ancient Egyptians and Romans valued roses too. They decorated their rooms with them, threaded them onto string and wore them as necklaces. For hundreds of years roses have been a symbol of love. Did you know that the expression 'under the rose' means that something is a secret?

Every year a rose festival is held in the Rose Valley in Bulgaria when the local people celebrate the rose picking. These roses are picked for the essential rose oil in them that is distilled and then used in perfumes and face creams and hair products. The petal-picking season begins with the rose festival at the end of May and the beginning of June. The petals are picked by hand, very early in the morning when the morning dew leaves the flowers at their most fragrant.

These oil-rich roses have been grown in the Rose Valley for hundreds of years. The valley is particularly good for growing roses because the temperature in February, when the buds form, is perfect. The sandy soil is just right, and the rain showers in May and June all contribute to producing the best fragrant roses from which to extract the oil.

About eight and a half thousand tons of rose petals are picked in Bulgaria every year to produce about two tonnes of rose oil. Most of that oil is exported all over the world to use as one of the ingredients to make perfume and other cosmetics. Seventy to eighty percent of the annual production of rose oil worldwide comes from the Bulgarian Rose Valley.

Over 1,000 petals of the *Rosa damascene* are crushed to produce one gram of oil. There are over 300 substances in that oil that are good for the skin.

Bulgarian rose oil is considered the best in the world, and costs €5,000 for one kilogram!

There is something Christlike in the way the rose petals are crushed when they are at their best to make the most precious, fragrant oil for all to enjoy! Jesus was crushed by our sins to cleanse us from every impurity so that we might be refined for His kingdom. Like this expensive and precious oil that blesses others with its rich perfume, we are called to share the beautiful perfume of God's love with others today. Will you?

PRAYER

Help me to spread cheer and joy to all I meet today. Amen.

The Water Lily (43)

THEME

We are spiritually nourished when we read God's word and spend time in prayer with Him.

BIBLE GEM

'They all ate the same spiritual food.'
1 Corinthians 10:3

YOU COULD USE

- A small water lily plant
- Enlarged photographs of water lilies

ILLUSTRATION

There is something extraordinarily beautiful about still water graced with water lilies floating on its surface as dragonflies with shimmering wings hover between them.

Besides their beautiful flowers of white, yellow or pink, water lilies are interesting in so many ways. I have overwatered many plants in my lifetime, and they have died. How does the water lily manage to grow and thrive in all that water? God made it with special adaptations. The water lily stem connects the floating leaves to the roots anchored at the bottom. The stems are especially long, allowing the plant to adjust to the changing water levels. The longer stems allow the plant to spread out on the water to get more sunlight and air. The stems are weak and floppy. They don't need to be strong, because they are supported by the water, which allows them to float.

And here is where they are so incredibly different to soil plants – because the roots cannot draw oxygen from the water, they absorb the oxygen through their leaves, which then travels down the tube-like stems to the roots. God thought of everything when He created our world, didn't He?

We need spiritual oxygen for our character to grow more like Jesus. Be like the water lily by absorbing God's love as you read your Bible and talk to Him in prayer every day. It will give you all the nourishment you need to be like Him!

PRAYER

Like the water lily absorbs oxygen, help me to absorb Your love. Amen.

The Pearl

THEME

Jesus is the priceless Pearl.

BIBLE GEM

'Again, the kingdom of heaven is like a merchant looking for fine pearls. When he found one of great value, he went away and sold everything he had and bought it.' *Matthew 13:45, 46*

YOU COULD USE

- Oyster shells
- A pearl or simulated pearl

ILLUSTRATION

[Hold up the shell and ask the children what it is. Once you have established that it is an oyster shell, pass around the pearl and ask them what it is. Ask them if they know whether there is any connection between the two.]

The pearl is called the 'jewel of the sea'. It is the only jewel not to come from the ground. Pearls are made from a type of material made by the oyster. Pearls are often white, or a pale colour. Some are black. Some are round; some are like flat discs; and others are irregular. Some pearls are tiny, like little seeds, while others are the size of a tennis ball, and there are all the other sizes between. Obviously, the very large pearls are extremely rare. The pearl called the Pearl of Lao Tzu, found in 1934, is as large as a basketball!

When a parasite bores into the outer shell, it damages it; the displaced nacre-producing cells from the mantle tissue start to produce nacre, and the pearl starts to form.

Pearl divers, usually very poor men, have looked for pearls since ancient times. A boat would take them out to sea to the pearl banks while it was still dark. The boat would anchor at sunrise and the pearl divers, working in pairs, would begin their day's work. They would jump into the water in a standing position, weighed down by rocks that carried them to the oyster bed. One would close his nose with his hands and the other would use a clip fastened to his nose. Once at the bottom, in sixty seconds they would gather as many oysters as they could and then slip them into a basket around their necks. The divers would tug at the rope, and the men in the boat would haul them up with their treasure.

They would take a few minutes to catch their breath before going down again. It is said that a single diver could collect 3,000 oysters a day.

The merchants would release the pearls from the oysters and would then sell them to dealers from all around the world.

Once there was a pearl merchant who saw the most amazing, beautiful pearl, which he wanted to buy, but the pearl diver refused to sell it to him. 'That pearl is priceless!' he said: and then he explained why.

'Two pearl divers, a father and son, went out to dive for oysters every day. Most days, there was little reward. They knew there was a part of the oyster bed where others had found big pearls, but it was dangerous, and the father would never let his son dive there. One day, the son went out alone to the dangerous part of the bed. He picked up the oyster with this pearl and swam up towards the boat, but he ran out of breath before he reached the surface, and he died. That boy was my son. He gave his life for that pearl. It is priceless.'

Jesus is a priceless Pearl, too. He gave His life for us. Are you willing to give up the things that distance you from Him so that you can live with Him forever?

PRAYER

Dear Jesus, You are my priceless Pearl. Like the merchant, I am willing to give up all that I own to live with You forever. Amen.

The Biggest Diamond in the World

sermon 45

THEME

As rough diamonds, God knows where our fault lines are. He will make us more like Him.

BIBLE GEM

'For it is God who works in you both to will and to work, for his good pleasure.' *Philippians 2:13 (WEB)*

YOU COULD USE

- A lump of coal or a charcoal briquette
- A diamond ring or clear shiny stone in a brooch

ILLUSTRATION

When you think of precious stones, which are the first stones you think of? [Allow the children to list a few.]

Whatever the stone, they are always prized for their beauty.

The most popular precious stone is the diamond. When cut and polished, it is clear with a brilliant shine. Because diamonds are the hardest natural objects on earth, nothing can leave scratches on them, apart from another diamond!

Most of the earth's natural diamonds are found in Africa. These stones are formed under intense pressure and heat about one hundred miles below the surface of the earth, and miners dig deep shafts in search of them.

The Star of South Africa was the first large diamond of gem quality found on the bank of the Orange River in South Africa in 1869 by an African shepherd boy. The boy exchanged it with a farmer for five hundred sheep, ten oxen and a horse. When people in Europe heard that there were big diamonds in Africa, they had dreams of finding a valuable diamond that would make them rich, and they rushed there to find their fortunes!

Many were disappointed. Most diamonds lie deep below the surface of the earth. The Star of Africa probably rose to the earth's surface through an eruption many years before.

The Cullinan diamond, from which the Great Star of Africa was cut, was found in 1905. It was the largest gem-quality rough diamond ever. It was even larger than the Star of South Africa! It was larger than a man's fist. It was given to King Edward VII, King of the United Kingdom of Great Britain and Ireland, for his sixty-sixth birthday as a token of loyalty from the people.

Mr Joseph Asscher, who lived in Amsterdam, was considered the best diamond cutter in the world at the time. He was asked to cut the stone. He studied it every day for three months to make sure it would have the most facets. It must have been very tense in the workroom when he struck the diamond with the cutter blade. BANG! Oh no! The cutter blade was broken, but fortunately the diamond was not damaged. He tried again, and this time it split perfectly along the fault line. The two stones were split into nine big stones and several smaller ones. Those nine stones are in the British Crown Jewels collection. The 'Great Star of Africa' is set in the Queen's Royal Sceptre, and the second one, slightly smaller, is centred at the front of the Imperial State Crown. Replicas are on display at the Tower of London.

Can you imagine how nervous Mr Asscher must have been? If he had cut the diamond in the wrong place, he could have destroyed it completely. By taking his time to study that diamond carefully for three months, he found out as much as he could so that the diamond would be shown to perfection. Through his painstaking work, those diamonds remain a symbol of royalty. You know, Jesus knows where our fault lines are too, and throughout our lives He carefully strikes them perfectly so that His brilliance will sparkle from every facet of our character.

Don't stay a rough diamond – allow the Master Diamond Cutter to polish you for His glory!

PRAYER

Dear Jesus, take this rough diamond; cut it and polish it to sparkle for You. Amen.

Salt **46**

THEME

Through the allegory of salt, Jesus encourages us to serve each other quietly and with humility.

BIBLE GEM

'Let your conversation be always full of grace, seasoned with salt, so that you may know how to answer everyone.' *Colossians 4:6*

YOU COULD USE

- The largest lumps of rough salt you can find
- A saltshaker filled with table salt

ILLUSTRATION

Did you know that I sometimes eat rocks? Yes, really, I do! In fact, I had some on my baked potato last night! You don't believe me? Let me show you. . . .

[Show the children some rock salt.]

When these rocks are finely ground, they look like this. [Show them table salt in a saltshaker.]

Now, do you know the name of these edible rocks? [Allow the children to answer.]

Did you know that salt is the only rock we can eat?

Too much of it is not healthy, but, when we consume the recommended amount, it is good for us and helps us in several ways. It aids digestion. It aids the transmission of nerve impulses. It helps our muscles to work properly. It helps the body to absorb potassium, which our bodies need for maintaining a healthy balance of fluids in the body. It offsets loss of water when we sweat a lot, or when we are feverish and ill.

Salt has many everyday uses – just a tiny pinch brings out the flavour in the food we eat. You can't see it in the food, but you can taste the difference it makes. It preserves food and stops it from going off.

The best type of sea salt contains many of the essential minerals the body needs.

Salt has been valued for hundreds and thousands of years. In the Middle Ages, it was so expensive, they called it 'white gold'.

During the Sermon on the Mount, Jesus told those who were listening to be like salt. By telling them that, He was encouraging them to bring out the flavour of those around them by serving them quietly with humility.

PRAYER

Dear Jesus, season my speech with words of kindness and encouragement. Amen.

The Dead Sea

THEME

We must share the Good News with others.

BIBLE GEM

'Quietly trust yourself to Christ your Lord, and if anybody asks why you believe as you do, be ready to tell him, and do it in a gentle and respectful way.' *1 Peter 3:15 (TLB)*

YOU COULD USE

- Pictures of the Dead Sea – there are plenty on the internet
- Two glasses of water, a bag of salt and a tablespoon
- Lotions, creams or scrubs from the Dead Sea – they are readily available at beauty counters in department stores. They are great, and you may want to try them!

ILLUSTRATION

The Dead Sea, in Israel, is situated just over one hundred miles south of the Sea of Galilee. 'Dead' seems such a strange name for a lake. We often hear the expression that 'water is life', but this body of water is named 'dead'. I wonder why they called it dead.

The Dead Sea is 'dead' because there is so much salt in it that not even fish or water plants can live in it. In fact, it is 8.6 times saltier than the ocean. If this glass represents the salt in the ocean [add one tablespoon of salt to it and stir] and this second glass represents the salt in the Dead sea [add eight and a half tablespoons of salt to it], you can see how much saltier it is. Unsurprisingly, that is why it is also called the Salt Sea.

The Dead Sea is not really a sea, but a lake: a salt lake. It is located at the lowest point on land. The reason it is so salty is because lots of water flows into it, but there are no streams or rivers flowing out of it.

One of the fun things about so much salt in the water is that this makes the water very dense. It is so dense that people can float in the water on their backs, even if they cannot swim! [Show pictures of people floating and reading a book.]

Some people have said that there are Christians who are like the Dead Sea. They only take, but never share Jesus' love with others. A lot of good flows in, but nothing flows out.

Jesus told us to be His witnesses. That means that we need to share the Good News with others and not keep it to ourselves. It means sharing what we have and making the world a better, kinder place for all. Sometimes we feel that we are too young or too shy to show others what Jesus is like. Our text tells us to put our trust in Jesus to help us to share God's love.

The Dead Sea may not provide water fit to drink, or give what we would expect from a lake, but the sea does 'give' in different ways. The water contains lots of different minerals that are good for healing some skin conditions and other health problems. Dead Sea salt is used in many beauty products that people use every day.

Asphalt is another of its gifts, in the black substance it spews up. Asphalt would have been used to make boats watertight in ancient times. We still use it today to fill potholes in our roads and to resurface our driveways. The lake isn't useless after all!

Could you be a healer like the water of the Dead Sea? Through your gentle and thoughtful words and actions, do you share the love of Jesus wherever you are? Go on, try it. . . . I dare you!

PRAYER

Dear Jesus, I love Sabbath School, church, and being with my friends. I have learned so much about You; now give me the courage to live what I have learned and to share it with others. Amen.

Clean Water

THEME

Jesus cleanses us from our sins.

BIBLE GEM

'I will sprinkle clean water on you, and you will be clean.' *Ezekiel 36:25*

YOU COULD USE

- An old white shirt or T-shirt (put it on before you talk to the children)
- A bowl with some damp soil or mud
- A glass of water

ILLUSTRATION

When I woke up this morning, I was so thirsty. I even felt a bit headachy. What do you think I did? [Show the children the glass of water and take a few sips.] Ah! Wonderful! That was so good! I feel better now!

Did you know that you could only survive for about three days without water? If you were in a hot car, it might be even less!

We all need water to survive. Our bodies are mostly water, which they need to work well. That is why it is good to be in the habit of carrying a bottle of water with you wherever you go.

We also need water to keep ourselves clean. That is why we bathe or shower every day and wash our hands regularly. Water on the outside helps us stay healthy, too.

Did you know that water is not only essential for us, but for all living things, like animals, plants and trees? That is why the water in our oceans covers about 70% of the planet. Some water floats in the air. Did you know that only about 3% of the earth's water is fresh water? Most of that fresh water is ice (glaciers), followed by the water under the ground and finally in lakes, rivers and streams?

Water is precious for life, and we need to protect it.

Jesus is like that precious water in our lives. Sometimes we do things we know we shouldn't do: we tell a little lie, because we do not want to get into trouble [take some of the soil or mud and smear it on the shirt] and it leaves a stain; it spoils who we are. Sometimes we take things that belong to someone else because we want them so badly [smear some more mud on the shirt]. Sometimes we are unkind to our friends. We may say mean words or stop playing with them [smear some more mud]. Sometimes we don't do our chores at home or we don't listen to our parents [smear some more] and we look a sorry sight, like this shirt. Would you wear a dirty shirt like this to church, or when you visit a friend? Of course not! The wrongs we do stain us, just like this shirt is stained.

Our text tells us that God promises to clean us with the water of life to wash away the stains from the wrong we do and to leave us sparkling clean. I need Jesus to wash me clean every day, and I love Him for doing it freely. Do you?

PRAYER

Dear Jesus, I am sorry for slipping up and for doing wrong. Thank You for washing away the stains this leaves on my life. Make me more like You! Amen.

Gold **(sermon 49)**

THEME

Never give up!

BIBLE GEM

'But he knows the way that I take; when he has tested me, I shall come forth as gold.' *Job 23:10*

YOU COULD USE

- Show the children any items of gold you may own
- Photographs of a bar/bars of gold
- A photograph of gold being smelted and/or poured

ILLUSTRATION

Guess what I am! Here are some clues . . .
- There are more than 400 references to me in the Bible!
- God told the Israelites to use me in my purest form to cover the furniture in the tabernacle.
- I was a gift one of the magi gave to Jesus when He was born.
- I am a metal.

Have you guessed what I am?

Gold!

[Show the children a wedding ring or another item of gold you may have, and then tell them these amazing facts about gold.]

Did you know that gold has been found on each of the continents of the world?

People discovered gold over 6,000 years ago. It has been highly valued ever since: not only for its colour, but also for many other reasons. Gold is very heavy; it does not rust or change due to age or the elements. It conducts heat and electricity. It is soft and malleable: that means it can be bent easily without breaking. Did you know that gold can be hammered into the thinnest sheets, called gold leaf? A pile of two hundred thousand sheets would only be 1 inch high! [You could compare this with the number of sheets of paper measuring 1 inch.] Just one ounce of gold can be stretched into a 60-mile-long thread!

Gold has many uses. Mostly it is used for jewellery. A typical wedding ring will weigh between three and seven ounces. It is also used in the glass of windows to stop the infrared rays from passing through them. This allows light into the room while keeping it cool. Gold is used to make electrical connectors in computers, because it does not rust.

Geologists believe that 80% of all the world's gold is still under the ground. It is also said that there are about 10 billion tons of gold in the ocean, but it is too expensive to mine the gold from the sea.

Because gold is such a valuable metal, most of the gold ever discovered is still in circulation.

I visited a gold mine once. Brave, strong men worked in it. Some of the gold mines go down as deep as 12,000 feet, where the temperature is very hot at 130 degrees Fahrenheit. I also watched a demonstration of the way gold is extracted from the rock and formed into gold bars the size of small loaves of bread. When seams of gold are seen in the rock, dynamite is used to break it up. That is scary, dangerous work! Then there are various processes to separate all the impurities from the gold. Finally, the gold is melted in ovens set at 1,064 degrees Celsius. It is then poured into moulds to set. Once set, it is held in huge, secure vaults.

In our text, Job hints at the harsh treatment gold goes through until it is pure. Life is like that too. We have hard knocks; friends don't like us any more; we struggle to understand something important at school; we make a bad mistake or a wrong choice and we are disciplined – but we learn from all these things. We go through the fire and come out as gold: gold that is not only beautiful to look at, but also precious, reliable and very useful!

Remember the gold bar and what it means to you every time you feel that life isn't fair!

PRAYER

Dear God, there are times I want to give up because I find it too hard to keep trying. Make me strong and willing to turn every failure into an opportunity. I want to be one of Your precious bars of gold. Amen.

The Rainbow Promise

sermon **50**

THEME

God keeps all His promises.

BIBLE GEM

'I establish my covenant with you: never again will all life be destroyed by the waters of a flood; never again will there be a flood to destroy the earth. . . . I have set my rainbow in the clouds, and it will be the sign of the covenant between me and the earth.' *Genesis 9:11-13*

YOU COULD USE

- Small rainbow images printed onto small stickers to give to each child.

ILLUSTRATION

How many of you have seen a real rainbow? What shape was it? What colours did you see? Is the rainbow an object? Can you touch it? When are you most likely to see a rainbow?

Rainbows are one of God's most special gifts to us, because they grace the sky with a promise He made to Noah and to us, for all time!

Do you know how rainbows form? You are likely to see one after the rain, but the sun must be behind you and the rain in front of you for the rainbow to appear. You can also see them in the early morning dew, or in the mist, or in the spray from the sprinkler on the lawn.

When the sun shines through the droplets of rain, the light is bent and separated into amazing colours. The main colours in a rainbow are red, orange, yellow, green, blue, indigo and violet. Although we only see these seven colours, the rainbow is made up of every colour there is, because sunlight is made up of all the colours!

When you see a rainbow from the ground it is always arced, and often we see it as half a circle. Rainbows are always circles of light: we just don't see the bottom half, unless we are in a plane looking down on the raindrops.

Rainbows can't be touched. They are not objects, so they can only be seen. For the older children, we call this an optical phenomenon.

The first sighting of a rainbow was after the flood Noah and his family had endured for many long days and nights. God spoke to Noah and promised him that He would never again destroy the whole earth by sending a flood. He told him that the rainbow would always be a reminder of this promise. In a way, the rainbow reminds us of God's glory and faithfulness to us. It reminds us that He keeps all His promises to us (2 Corinthians 1:20).

Have you made promises you have kept? Have you made promises you have broken? How did you feel? On the other hand, has someone made a promise to keep a secret that they then broke? How did you feel? Did you feel as if they had broken your trust?

God has never broken His promises to humans. We can safely trust Him. Every time you see a rainbow, will you remember God's promises to you? Will you promise to be His loving child forever?

PRAYER

Dear Father God, we love seeing the rainbow in the sky after the rain. We know that it isn't just a reflection of light through the rain, but also a symbol of Your promise to us to protect us and to keep us safe from harm. Thank You, in Jesus' name. Amen.

Fool's Gold

sermon 51

THEME

Seek the genuine. 'All that glitters is not gold.'

BIBLE GEM

'Now devote your heart and soul to seeking the LORD your God.' *1 Chronicles 22:19*

YOU COULD USE

• Examples of pyrite

ILLUSTRATION

A long time ago, in 1576, an English 'pirate' found some black rock with golden crystals on Kodlunarn Island, Canada. He was convinced he had found his fortune, and many people back in England gave him enough money to extract 200 tons of sparkly rock.

By now the Queen was so excited, she sent him back with a fortune to bring back more ore. Two years later he shipped back 1,350 tons of ore.

But disaster struck! The ship was wrecked and some of the ore was lost. The ore that was saved was sent to Dartford to be smelted. Can you imagine how angry the Queen must have been when she found out that the 'gold' wasn't gold at all? In the smelting process it had decomposed into a black dust!

It may have looked like gold, but it wasn't even a metal. Lots of people have been fooled by this 'fool's gold' over the years.

While gold is a brassy metal, it always looks like metal. Fool's gold, or pyrite, looks like rock. Gold diggers soon learned to do some tests to be certain that their treasure was the real thing, that it was gold.

They would do the glitter test. You see, gold shines, but it does not glitter. Because 'fool's gold' is made up of crystals, it sparkles and glitters.

Then there was the hardness test. While gold is soft, and dents and bends easily, pyrite is hard, and shatters if hammered. Gold does not shatter.

The final test was the acid test. They would put their treasure in nitric acid. The gold stayed unchanged, but pyrite dissolved!

As children who love Jesus, we could do some tests on ourselves too. Remember the saying, 'All that glitters is not gold'? Are we all glitter on the inside, pretending to be gold – or are we real gold shining for Him?

When we go through the hardness test, are we soft, allowing Jesus to shape us – or are we like fool's gold that shatters?

Finally, if we go through the 'acid test', are we unchanged – or do we dissolve into nothing?

Daniel, a young boy who was not afraid to stay true to God when it would have been easier to give in just a little, was an example of a child made of gold. Like a nugget of gold, he shone; he never shattered under pressure or dissolved into nothing.

When we truly seek God, we will be His nuggets of true gold!

PRAYER

Dear Father God, it is so easy to be impressed by glittering 'fool's gold', and to waste our time looking for it. Help us to be genuine, to be Your treasured nuggets of gold. Amen.

The Volcano

THEME

Soon we will go home with Jesus to live with Him in heaven.

BIBLE GEM

'My Father's house has many rooms; if that were not so, would I have told you that I am going there to prepare a place for you? And if I go and prepare a place for you, I will come back and take you to be with me that you also may be where I am.' *John 14:2, 3*

YOU COULD USE

- Photographs of volcanic eruptions
- Samples of different types of volcanic rock (if available) to explain what they are

ILLUSTRATION

Earlier this month a volcano on the island of Stromboli in the Mediterranean erupted with two very powerful explosions. A local priest said it was like a rain of fire falling from the sky. Many tourists fled to the sea, and navy boats came to their rescue. Volcanoes are like giant chimneys or funnels that reach down to the centre of the earth, allowing the magma, red-hot liquid rocks and built-up gases to explode and escape. As the magma or lava hardens, it cools.

On 20 March 2010, I was visiting a small school in Galway, Ireland. The children were lovely, the head teacher was lovely and so were all the teachers. It was good to be there, but then something happened, and I just wanted to jump on a plane and get home as soon as possible, but it wasn't going to be easy. . . .

In Iceland Mt Eyjafjallajökull, an ice-capped volcano, had erupted and spread its volcanic ash across the British Isles. I had never seen the sky look like that before. All flights back to England were cancelled, as were all the airports everywhere. I took a train to Dublin – it was packed with passengers, many wanting to get to the seaport to take the ferry to Wales. And I was one of them. The crossings were fully booked, and I had to watch and wait until the ferry I was booked on sailed into view. That was when I began to feel a little happier. I was on my way home. But that was only the beginning of the very strange journey. Once at Holyhead, I dashed to get the train I had booked. It was packed; someone else was sitting in my booked seat. 'You'll just have to stand,' the conductor said. Suitcases were piled up everywhere, and we bumped into each other far too many times as we rattled down the track. It took four train journeys, standing all the way, and more than 24 hours to finally reach home.

The Bible doesn't mention volcanoes by name, but it does describe them, along with earthquakes, which often set them off. Earthquakes and volcanic eruptions are described along with the way life will be just before Jesus comes again. They often sound terrifying. Getting caught up in them must be frightening.

For me, the eruption was all about going home. I could not rest until the journey was over and I was safely where I belonged. It reminded me that we are really on our journey home to be forever with Jesus. Is that what is foremost in our minds, or are we so disturbed by the terrifying events happening around us that we can't think about 'going home' or what it means? In the words of a song we don't sing very often any more, remember, 'Anywhere with Jesus I can safely go. . . .' Have a safe journey home, folks! See you there!

PRAYER

Dear Jesus, thank You for leading us home. Amen.

Also available in this range from Autumn House are two great books by
Anne Pilmoor and Karen Holford.

52

5-minute

SERMONS

for kids

Anne Pilmoor

52 WAYS

to Parent

happy

children

Karen Holford

Why not share them with your
precious little ones and inspire them with God's love?

Autumn House